Gordon S
Something Left Behind

Something Left Behind © 2001 by Pamela S. Allyn
Gordon Solie ... Something Left Behind © 2004 by Pamela S. Allyn

Front cover photo credit: *Tampa Tribune*—Fred Bellet/Tribune file photo (1997)

Copyright 2004 by Pamela S. Allyn

All rights reserved. No part of this book may be reproduced in any form or by any electronic or mechanical means, including information storage and retrieval systems without permission in writing from the publisher, except by a reviewer who may quote brief passages in a review.

Florida Media, Inc.
801 Douglas Avenue, Suite 100
Altamonte Springs, FL 32714
407-816-9596

ISBN 0-9763062-290000

Dedication

If Gordon Solie were alive today, we believe he would have dedicated his writings to: the fans for allowing him into their homes, the wrestlers for respecting him, "Cowboy" Luttrall for hiring him, Frank Dery for providing a big career break, Eddie Graham for briefing him, Don Curtis for sustaining him, Tom McEwen for advising him on writing, and Coach John Heath for educating him on wrestling holds and physical terminologies.

Bob and Pam Allyn

Acknowledgements

A special thank you to those of you who graciously shared your time, material, knowledge or likeness:

Terry Allen, Jameson Allyn, Toni Anker, Bill Apter, Russ Bennedict, Brian and Toni Blair, Jack and Jan Brisco, Mike Clark, The Coca-Cola Company, Buddy Colt, Don and Dotty Curtis, Wayne Fariss, Dory and Marti Funk, Jr., Terry Funk, Jim Gallagher, Gordon Solie Enterprises, Inc., Suzanne Hennon, Sir Oliver Humperdink, Tony Hunter, Paul Jones, Steve Keirn, Norman Keitzer, Karl Lauer, Timothy Leahy, Dennis Lee, Scooter Lesley, the late Horace "Hoss" Logan (The Louisiana Hayride), Paul MacArthur, Johnny Maddox, Jimmy Marshall, Bill Martin, John McAdam, Tom McEwen, Bugsy McGraw, The Fabulous Moolah, Mike Mooneyham, Phyllis Musgrave, Sonny Myers, Mark Nulty, Bill Otten, Diamond Dallas Page, Frank Page (The Louisiana Hayride), Joe Pedicino, Ed Pendino, Bob Phillips, Jerry Prater, Harley Race, Jim Ross, Rob Russen, Bob Ryder, Stu and Bonnie (Watson) Schwartz, David Skolnick, Rick Stephenson, Michael Steward, John Stewart, Gaye Swenson, Rich Tate, Scott Teal, Mike Tenay, Les Thatcher, Gary Theroux, Ronald C. Thomas, Jr., Bob Vallee, Bill Watts, Tedd Webb, Jack Welch, Sarah Wilhite, and Don Woods.

We appreciate the information available online for verifying title histories: "Pro-Wrestling Title Histories" (www.wrestling-titles.com); "Solie's Vintage Wrestling" (www.solie.org); and the originators of much of the title history compilation, Royal Duncan and Gary Will, authors of *Wrestling Title Histories*.

Preface

The day was August 5, 2000. Six hundred people gathered at a Tampa church to pay their respect to the late Gordon Solie, the "Dean of Professional Wrestling Announcers." After the memorial service, a petite dishwater-blonde-haired woman approached professional wrestler Scott Hall. She had never met Scott, but her nieces, Samantha and Nicole, were asking to meet him. One glance at her and Scott remarked, "My God, you have his eyes!" The observation brought a slight smile to Pam's otherwise grief-stricken face. She heard similar comments throughout her life. "You look like Gordon spit you out of his mouth," people would say.

Shared physical characteristics were one thing. More important was the spiritual bond between Gordon and Pam, a bond known only to fathers and their daughters. It was a bond that passed the tests of time, distance and even death. Pam and her father had nine years together until they were separated by a divorce. The following year, Pam's mother remarried, taking her children away from Tampa, Fla., to Bloomington, Ill. No more jumping into Dad's arms when he came home from work. No more tagging along when Dad promoted a stock car race or a wrestling event. No more fashion shows with him or riding on a float in the Gasparilla Parade. No more great bedtime stories from Dad. In fact, there would be no more Gordon for years to come, other than a few restaurant rendezvous during summer vacations.

In the long periods of their physical separation, Gordon took a serious interest in a substitute child. He named the new child "Professional Wrestling," and he nurtured the youngster for many years. Late in his career, he had his "original firstborn," as Gordon called Pam, back in his life and it was a sight to behold! Gordon and Pam spoke for hours at a time trying to make up for the lost years. Tears flowed down Gordon's cheeks as he uttered, "I'm so sorry." Sorry for the missing years, but joyful for the second chance. Pam also became a new source of pride for Gordon. He commented often about her family and career accomplishments, but he was most impressed with her unconditional love.

The recognition of her devotion led Gordon to a decision. He revealed his conclusion one afternoon while relaxing with Pam and her husband, Bob Allyn. Gordon turned to Pam and spoke, "I'm going to leave all of my writings to you. You'll know what to do with them." After his death, the writings took a backseat for more than a year while Pam took care of her duties as one of the personal representatives for Gordon's estate. Finally, she pulled out Gordon's personal writing files and perused them with Bob. The files contained a prelude and an outline for a wrestling book that Gordon never wrote, along with short stories, prose, articles, event programs and photos. By combining their photos and research with Gordon's writing files, Bob and Pam developed more than 2,200 files for the book project. Together they interviewed wrestlers, referees, managers, media personnel and some of Gordon's close friends.

After 35 months of inquiries, Bob and Pam's plan began to take shape. They intertwined more than 160 photos with a portion of Gordon's previously unpublished writings. *Gordon Solie ... Something Left Behind* is not only a tribute to Gordon, but also to the fans and athletes who shared moments with one of America's finest broadcasters.

Table of Contents

*All writings herein were written by Gordon Solie unless otherwise noted.
Picture captions and other notations written by Robert and Pamela Allyn.*

PREFACE .... page 4

INTRODUCTION.. page 9

CHAPTER 1   EARLY AIR WAVES .... page 12
                 The Good Life .... page 16
                 Togetherness? .... page 22

CHAPTER 2   WRITINGS FROM THE ROAD .... page 23
                 Silver and Green... page 23
                 The Fair .... page 24
                 Dyna and the Truck .... page 27
                 28 Seconds .... page 32
                 Remembering... page 34
                 A Failed Experiment... page 35
                 Big Daddy Takes a Walk .... page 36
                 The Lady of St. Regis.. page 38

CHAPTER 3   THE MERGER: TELEVISION AND WRESTLING .... page 41
                 One Good Try .... page 41
                 Sirens of Life .... page 45
                 The Resilient Man .... page 52
                 Self-Menagerie .... page 66
                 Sunday Morning .... page 74

CHAPTER 4	LESSONS	page 75
	Power Buttons	page 75
	Picayune, Mississippi	page 84
	The Birds	page 84
CHAPTER 5	ACCEPTANCE	page 85
	Flying in '64	page 85
CHAPTER 6	STRICTLY WRESTLING	page 93
	Grudge Match	page 93
	Ted	page 96
	The Real Prophets	page 106
	They and Me	page 109
	The Narrow Road	page 110
	The Great Thinkers	page 114
	The Dare	page 115
CHAPTER 7	STRICTLY RACING	page 121
	Tortured Rubber	page 121
	The Finale	page 152
CHAPTER 8	HEAD SHOTS	page 153
	The Fascia Sea	page 153
	Head Lines	page 157
	Existence	page 161
	Pure Mediocrity	page 165
	Roses	page 166
	Parking Lot Egos	page 167

CHAPTER 9	MASTER OF THE INTERVIEW	page 177
	The Champion	page 177
	Unequals	page 180
	Prime Gone	page 187
	John Thomas	page 197
CHAPTER 10	ANOTHER ROAD TO ROME	page 205
	One Week from Rome	page 205
	A Fairy Tale	page 207
	To Henry's Pond	page 211
	The Game	page 211
CHAPTER 11	STARTING ANEW	page 212
	Too Much	page 212
	Post Wrestling Depression	page 217
	Prelude	page 218
	Full Circle	page 219
	The Awares	page 219
	Hope	page 219
	Lord of the Microphone (excerpt) by Bill Apter	page 220
	Something Left Behind by Jameson Parker Allyn	page 221

Introduction

"Ironical" is a word that comes to mind when considering the chosen field of the late Gordon Solie. In the 1940s, the expectations of young males raised in well-to-do American homes did not usually include plans for careers in professional wrestling or stock car racing. Even Gordon's Southwest High School classmates in Minneapolis, Minn., prophesized him in a white-collar position such as a round table mediator for NBC. The eyebrows of his mother and adopted father certainly rose when Gordon was first referred to as "The Black Leather Jacket Announcer."

The choice *was* Gordon's. As a young man breaking into the 1950 Tampa radio business, Gordon observed an injustice in the local media. The front page of local sports sections featured events such as lawn tennis matches with 15 or 20 people cheering on the competitors. Stock car races and wrestling matches with thousands of fans showing up weekly were principally ignored by the press. Gordon's goal was clear; he would make his mark by changing the image of professional wrestling and stock car racing in the Tampa Bay area.

Gordon learned about stock car racing by competing as an amateur chauffeur on Florida's Suncoast and announcing outdoors at tracks throughout the United States. He learned about wrestling by climbing in the ring with professional wrestlers John Heath, Eddie Graham and Don Curtis. He conducted radio interviews in Tampa with stock car drivers, boxers and pro wrestlers. In his spare time, Gordon often visited the Tampa library to learn more about the human anatomy. Fans and media were soon awed when Gordon Solie described the maneuvers of a wrestling match or called the action for a 200-lap late model stock car race.

The local media could no longer ignore racing or wrestling in Tampa because they couldn't ignore Gordon Solie! Gordon was at the center of major stock car races and charity events, and his face along with a distinct voice were found on the No. 1 television show coming out of the state, *Championship Wrestling from Florida (CWF)*.

Wrestling fans had a new icon. With *CWF*'s high network ratings, the viewers' support was evident, and the fans' loyalty to Gordon was again apparent at live shows when he signed more autographs than the wrestlers. The wrestlers didn't complain. They praised Gordon for his apt description of their physical attributes and precise moves executed on their opponents in the ring. They respected Gordon for "putting them over" to the fans and shining the light on them during his "deadpan" style interviews.

In 1972, Gordon began hosting an additional television show, *Georgia Championship Wrestling,* out of Atlanta, Ga. Around a decade later, Jay West wrote in *TV Wrestling-Dumont to Cable*: "Today on the Turner Satellite Cable System, the weekly 2-hour *Georgia Championship Wrestling* show is received by over 10 million cable homes in 48 states making it the most watched wrestling program in the country." Gordon had arrived as the No. 1 professional wrestling commentator in the world.

When Gordon wasn't speaking words into a microphone he was busy recording them on paper. Words were one of Gordon's passions in life. Early in his career, Gordon wrote as a "stringer" for Florida newspapers: Lakeland's *The Ledger, The Tampa Times, The Tampa Tribune, The Temple Terrace Times* and *LaGaceta,* a trilingual newspaper in Ybor City. While handling the public relations work for "Cowboy" Luttrall's Deep South Sports wrestling promotion, Gordon wrote each week for Tampa's *Sportscaster* in a column entitled *Sports Shots with Solie.* Ads and press releases written by Gordon for stock car races, wrestling matches, charity events or daredevil feats appeared consistently in publications throughout his career.

After the Florida Bar twice honored Gordon with the "Radio Editorial of the Year," he went on to write and produce his own radio show. Event coordinators called on Gordon to write athletes' biographies for televised sports entertainment and documentaries.

If a good idea or story popped into Gordon's head in a private moment, it was recorded on a cocktail napkin, hotel stationary or a legal pad. He saved his personal writings over the years in the form of prose and short stories. Most of his writings are based on real life experiences, and Gordon clearly identifies himself in the yarns. In some of the tales, however, Gordon opted to change names, including his own. This volume also displays some of Gordon's fictional work. The first selection written by Gordon appears next.

One has a truly great problem in trying to destroy materialism. To rid you of the things that count so much to many, takes more than just a little amount of guts. One, out of necessity, has to earn some sort of living. The mediocre people have only, one, great ability. They are the gatherers, the collectors, the rulers and the damnation of any society. What difference who rules? One mediocre form of government is as good as the other. Are all of the conveniences we have good? I think not. We are beginning to lose touch with reality. Who cares whether these thoughts of mine are ever printed? The important premise is they have been written. Whether anyone else ever reads them or not is transcended by the fact that I have expressed my own truisms. There is a great temptation to join again the throngs who no longer fight for individuality, who grovel at the sign of a dollar, who will prostitute themselves and ideas for the sake of an extra ten. I'll bet some don't even need the extra ten. Pity the poor man … he is happy … he thinks he is right. Don't pity me … I know … I will never be happy … I will never understand. I will always be searching for that indefinable intangible substance that makes a life complete. I have known the child who could complete my life by her very existence. I have known more of life than I have ever thought possible before.

Family photo

Gordon and daughter Pamela in 1957

CHAPTER ONE
Early Air Waves

Born 1929 Adopted 1938 Legal Name Change 1961
Jonard Frank Labak* Jonard Pierre Sjoblom Gordon T. Solie

Family photo

Gordon Solie's "Golden Voice of The South" was first recorded through a new device called a Speak-a-Phone in 1933 at Bernstein's Department Store in Minneapolis, Minn. The 5-year-old Gordon (pictured above) initiated his future career by entertaining his family. When sports radio programs aired at the Sjoblom house, Gordon called his own play-by-play.

*Labak, traced back to the early Galicians of Poland was also spelled Labiak.

Family photo

Gordon (above left) and a pal created buildings for toy cars and airplanes from a deck of playing cards. A fascination with autos, especially the skill of high-speed stock car drivers, stayed with Gordon throughout his life, while airplanes became his favorite mode of transportation.

Family photo

During his secondary school years at Southwest High, Gordon chose radio as a major. Back then he answered to the nickname, "Josie." He ran the school PA system and participated in several high school stage productions as well as drama workshops at local radio stations in the 1940s.

Family photo *Family photo*

A confident 16 year old   1947 High School Graduation

Above left, Gordon is pictured as the suave teen that snuck off to attend stock car races in the Minneapolis area. In the photo, above right, Gordon is attired as the young man who delivered his high school graduation baccalaureate. His charismatic personality earned him the titles of "Biggest Flirt," "Best Talker" and "Best Line" from his high school classmates. Gordon's sister, Gaye, appeared with him below.

Family photo

Something Left Behind

The Good Life

The embodiment of good living is exercise and mental gymnastics.
When one has completed a day of healthy activity
And then proceeds to read or indulge in stimulation by conversation;
Then one is bound to gain every bit of living available in life.
(Army Air Force 1950)

Gordon earned his Sergeant's stripes in the United States Army Air Force 7th Geodetic Squadron as a VHF radio technician on the P51s. The Geodetic Squad was the forerunner for early radar detection systems. His initial dream was to enter the service and learn the trade of encrypting or decoding messages. A change in Gordon's goals began while stationed at Barksdale Air Force Base in Shreveport, La. During a weekend job at radio station KWKH and its sponsored show *The Louisiana Hayride,* Gordon was influenced by country music stars like Hank Williams Sr., Miss Kitty Wells, Johnny and Jack with the Tennessee Boys, and Slim Whitman.

Family photo

Gordon is pictured (above left) at the Hollywood Bowl with a fellow U.S. Army Air Force officer.

Gordon (back right) and Army Air Force buddies

Something Left Behind

Family photo

As part of his tour of duty, Gordon spent 17 months stationed in Okinawa.

Family photo

Gordon's post-military career, under the G.I. Bill, began in 1950 at WEBK Radio in Ybor City, Tampa's Latin Quarter. Shortly after Wayne Fariss hired him to host a rhythm and blues segment, Gordon sold sponsorships for his own show to interview local professional athletes. He first met promoter "Cowboy" Luttrall when seeking permission to interview professional wrestlers on the air. Not only did "Cowboy" agree, he soon hired Gordon as his ring announcer and later asked Gordon to take over the public relations duties, as well.

Family photo

Chaz Roye, Gordon, fellow station employee and Wayne Fariss at WEBK Radio

From the Gordon Solie Collection

Gordon in the squared circle with two young fans

From the Gordon Solie Collection

In 1952, Gordon (far right) joined Milt Spencer (above left) on a sports radio show for Tampa's WFLA Radio. They remained close friends for more than 30 years. Milt later became first vice president of the National Sportscasters and Sportswriters Association.

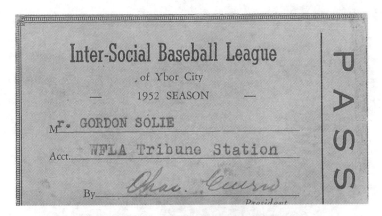

From the Gordon Solie Collection

Al Lopez, one of Tampa's favorite sons and a Major League Baseball Hall of Fame inductee, played in the Inter-Social Baseball League before his 1928 debut with the Brooklyn Dodgers. The Inter-Social Baseball League was just a group of working-class guys enjoying the game of baseball.

Gordon (below) moved his family of four to Plant City, Fla., and began broadcasting for WFLA's sister station, WPLA.

From the Gordon Solie Collection

Center stage at the microphone (below) was Gordon in 1953 with musicians at Plant City Park in Plant City, Fla. Lonzo and Oscar, the last two on the right, performed on WSM Radio in Nashville and kept audiences laughing at the Grand Ole Opry. The song "I'm My Own Grandpa" became synonymous with their names.

From the Gordon Solie Collection: photo by H. E. Perkins

Togetherness?

The curious medicinal odor and taste of scotch

A hot summer afternoon

A sheet of white paper

A portable typewriter

Do these make up the writer?

A car half paid for

A small home one tenth paid for

A wife

2 children

Church on Sunday

Does this make up living?

Pseudo friends over for a barbeque

Mental passes made by husbands

False laughter by the group

Each worried about his own problems

Each cheating a little on his taxes

Each defeated in his own way

No one admitting it

This is togetherness?

CHAPTER TWO
Writings from the Road

Silver and Green

A bell chimed, the sun shone, a quiet breeze,
Voices muted by granite walls, sang the doxology.
Across the thoroughfare, the Carneys talked.
Two forms of worship on this Sabbath day,
One for Christendom,
One for Silver and Green.
Which is right?
Which is wrong?
Scant honest in one,
Honest of at least thought in the other.
Ah! Religion has many forms.
Which to choose?

The Fair

Noises in the crisp night
"Pitch till ya win"
"Watch the crazy ball"
"Show your muscles … ring the bell"
Eager faces-eyes alive with glitter and flash
Of the red, white, black and yellow painted
Signs of the joints, cries of happiness when a winner was made
Embarrassed grins when the young swain
Tried his luck at pitching to win a teddy bear
Bloodshot eyes of the soaks watching nothing,
Seeing nothing.
Lined, tanned faces of farmers uncomprehending,
Spending their silver and green.
The eyes of the teenster looking for a pickup.
The pickup trying to remain demure.
The tired facades of the Carney, pitching, wheeling,
Cajoling and pitching.
The odor of fried onions,
The smell of hot black coffee
The small shouts of "George, you won!"
The tired cops.
Long hours-short pay-tired feet-too much traffic
Too many drunks-not enough pay.
Firecrackers exploding in spasmodic bursts.
Faces-some flushed-some blank
Kind-drunk-cynical
Faces, faces, faces, a carnival's composition
Faces-silver and green.

From the Gordon Solie Collection

In the late 1950s, Gordon was considered the best outdoor announcer in the United States. Wrestling was seasonal in Tampa at the time, and Aut Swenson's Thrillcade became Gordon's summer announcing employment for three consecutive years. The Thrillcade traversed the United States, parts of Canada and Mexico. Thrillcade performers entertained audiences with daredevil auto and motorcycle stunts inspiring future Bobby Knievels.

From the Gordon Solie Collection

Dyna and the Truck

The applause died away and once again the audience became hushed and expectant. The announcer lifted his microphone and looked toward the track. Jimmy James nodded his head and moved out to the center of the track, crash helmet in hand. The announcer began to speak, "For the finale for our show tonight, the most dangerous, difficult, sensationally, spectacular, suicidal stunt ever attempted on any thrill show! You are going to watch a Thrillcade daredevil attempt to hurtle this new pickup truck 80 feet through space from ramp to ramp over the back of our elephant! Ladies and Gentlemen, you now see the daredevil, who is going to attempt that leap, standing before you adjusting his crash helmet."

While the announcer was addressing the audience, Jimmy moved easily into position directly in front of the center section of the grandstand. He put his hand to his chest in almost a depreciating gesture, although he was actually adjusting his hearing aid. He lost the hearing sense years before when rolling a car on another show. Battery acid had run down his face into his nose and ears when his Junker hadn't gone all the way over. His face, though still handsome, was beginning to show more and more each year the ravages of bumps, cuts, and hard, fast living. He held his head slightly to one side and listened as the announcer continued, "And now Jimmy James will get into that pickup truck!" At this point, Larry O'Brien slid the pickup into position immediately behind Jimmy. "But one moment, Ladies and Gentlemen, as you know I never call for a hand for any of our daredevils before they attempt any feat, however, because of the dangers involved, may I direct you to deliver a rousing ovation to Jimmy James at this time? Ladies and Gentlemen, the 'Dean of Daredevils,' Jimmy James!"

Jimmy looked up, raised his left hand in a quick salute and trotted to the pickup. The audience reacted in the manner that they always do with a burst of applause, a volley of whistles and scattered cheers. A dozen ghosts of bygone days hovered in the shadows beyond the lights of the grandstand, wavered expectantly, and nodded their gray-like heads.

The pickup was light blue in body, one of the new creations in color designed by some bright young engineer. It actually resembled the sky on its brightest day. The front of the hood proper was covered with deep crimson flames tinged with a yellowish orange. Black tires with white sidewalls and shiny chrome completed the mechanical picture. It glistened slightly in the false glare of the floodlights.

"And now, Jimmy James is in the pickup. Jimmy, be sure to adjust your safety belt properly, and will the attendant standing by make sure the door is properly locked?" James could be seen pulling sharply on the safety belt. O'Brien shut the door with a flourish that was a little unnecessary. "And now, Jimmy James, are you ready?" Jimmy answered with a wave of the hand out the left hand window of the pickup truck. "Good luck, Jimmy! Good luck, indeed!"

From the Gordon Solie Collection

Three thousand people sat hushed, waiting, expectant as the blue pickup truck picked up speed and moved down the track in reverse order toward the number four turn. It became a shadowy form as it moved past the lights into the ever-consuming darkness of night. You could still make out the silhouette of the vehicle as it began to turn around deep in the number three turn.

Jimmy pulled sharply to the left and stopped. He made a hurried last-minute check. The jerubs were ready; he finished turning the truck around, checked his speedometer, pressed down on the accelerator, and watched the needle climb with one eye while he negotiated the turn. The red marker moved up to the prescribed speed … so far, so good. The announcer continued to explain what was going to occur. "The ramp to ramp leap was originated years ago by the great Lucky Teeter. Only a few short months ago, Lucky Teeter tragically lost his life while attempting a ramp to ramp jump. And yes, even Lucky Teeter never attempted to jump a pickup truck and certainly never attempted to jump any vehicle over the back of a live elephant. Jimmy James is the only stunt man alive today in the world to attempt such a leap. And now watch carefully as Jimmy James begins to move down the track to this spectacular suicidal leap over the back of Dancing Dyna, our Elephant."

The truck began to move now out of the murky light of semi-night, faster and faster it rolled toward turn number four. Jimmy swung out of the number four turn and lined up with the take-off ramp. He seemed to approach too fast, he checked his speed ... perfect, the wind whistled through the vents. He pressed the horn button which ignited the jerubs, they exploded and sent a shower of silver from the chrome tail pipe extensions. The audience gasped quickly! It was unexpected.

The announcer, by now, was shouting in a fever pitch, shouting to Jimmy to watch his speed, he was coming too fast ... "Watch your speed Jimmy. Watch it!"

The elephant looked down the track and saw the truck approaching, she began to move uneasily and then she began to trumpet. Jimmy felt the front wheels hit the take off ramp and watched the nose of the truck swing upward quickly. Suddenly he was in space.

From the Gordon Solie Collection

The audience was on its feet shouting and then he hit the opposite side of the ramp, too far over, recover, not too much … that's better. Now the hard crunch of the springs hitting the frame … the hard bounce … the lesser bounce … on the track now, brakes … not too much … that's it … and now the truck was rolling smoothly on the clay surface of the track again.

The audience roared its approval as the announcer suddenly cracked through the noise and asked for silence … then in a hushed voice he continued …"Ladies and Gentlemen, let's have complete silence … let's not have a sound in the entire amphitheater until this man returns." James meantime, was slowing, turning the pickup around in the number one turn … silence hung like the gray morning fog hangs over the roadway waiting to be broken.

"Let's wait until this man returns, so that he too may hear the ovation that he so richly deserves. Let's wait now until you see the door of that pickup truck open and then … let's tear the roof off the grandstand!"

James gunned the engine just a shade as he pulled up in front of the grandstand. He looked through the glass at the people waiting so expectantly. "Wonder what they'd do if I didn't get out," he thought as he reached for the door handle. He stepped out smiling broadly, his arm raised in a salute. Before he made it out the door, however, the sound enveloped him. There was a roar and a rush of applause as the announcer continued, "For Jimmy James, the bravest, wisest, most courageous stuntman in the world today … the 'Dean of Daredevils'."

With the sounds beginning to fade the announcer once again lifted the mike to his lips. "And now, Ladies and Gentlemen, on behalf of Aut Swenson and on behalf of every member of the Thrillcade troupe, this is Gordon Solie saying bye-bye, and remember when you do buy … buy Ford." He put the microphone down and the music from the sound car rose high in the air, giving impetus to the pushing crowd that was disappearing toward the exits.

James, who was also track manager, was in his trailer now changing clothes while the ramp hands began the task of tearing down ramps, loading the trucks and the thousand other details that go into getting the units on the road to the next fair date. This was the fat time of the year. The still dates were over, and the show was booked solidly every night for the next three months. Swenson was still in the secretary's office counting the receipts when Solie walked in to give him a report on how the show fared.

"We had a swinger tonight Aut," were Solie's opening comments. Swenson sometimes acted like he didn't quite comprehend the manner of conversation used by his emcee. But once you knew Aut, you knew that this was a general attitude of his that had cost many a competitor a good spot. Feigning a lack of comprehension can cause an opponent to let his guard down. And the minute you let your guard down with Swenson, you've had it. "Swell Gordie," were the only comments from Swenson, though he smiled broadly.

James pulled his shirt off and viewed his tired body. The chest that once was powerful and muscular was now soft and flabby. His stomach was distended from too much beer and easy living. His legs were thin and aged, showing his age as much as the rest of his torso. He was tired. He wondered how much longer he could go on … he wondered. How many more jumps before time caught him in its web of disuse and waste?

He pulled on his trousers and buttoned his shirt. He had better get out and get those stupid ramp hands moving. He opened the door to his trailer and looked out toward the track; the boys were loading the ramp truck and squaring away the other equipment that had to be carried from date to date.

He stepped off the stairs to the trailer and walked over to help Ken load the two motorcycles onto his truck. The pickup was holding up well, he thought, as he picked his way over the uneven ground of the infield. James sounded tired as he spoke to Ken, "Well, we'll load it and get rolling." Day in, day out, they moved. Each town had its own problems regarding the track … the men … and the equipment. And so life goes on.…

28 Seconds

The crowd roared and cheered.
The rider threw both arms high in the air.
He shouted his answer.
The crowd didn't hear.
Already they were listening to the announcer as
He introduced the next event.
The rider's moment of glory was over.
Back to work.
Tear down the loop.
Load the ramps.
Day in day out … for four months,
He was a hero for 28 seconds.
The length of time it took to hurtle down an inclined track
Into the air … 3 summersaults … a jarring landing on the
Receiving ramp … out of the juggernaut … face the crowd….
The crowd roared and cheered.

From the Gordon Solie Collection

Remembering

The day I first saw them,
Each an individual, each a part of you.
I held her hand as she like you
Looked to the sea and longed.
A wistful, searching look for such an infant.
Ah, the ageless wonder of a child's eyes.
I miss you … and him and her.
I miss all three.

A Failed Experiment

Love left me last night as suddenly as it had come

In one breath, I no longer loved you

For a moment I felt nothing, and then this became the same as all the others

The same phony ending, the passion dying, the regret and the cynical to self remarks

It's all the same

And then I sat and tried to place my mixture of thoughts together in some form of order

It isn't the same … there is a difference

But now then is it loyalty? Sympathy? Passion?

I think not.

I still love though the love that left will never return

But the love I know is a longer lasting sensation

A need of somewhat a different nature.

I don't know if you will note the difference in my being or not…

I rather think you sensed it coming yesterday

But couldn't describe what it was

The almost frantic I love you, I love you, and I love you, pouring from your mouth

Were, I think, in a way to tell me that you sensed it too and had to comfort me…

Or was it necessary for you to hear the words over and over again

To attempt confirmation in your mind?

I do not beg to know … but to know is a necessity.…

To say one word and mean another would be cruel and

This I know you cannot do.

What is the answer … tell me now … if done … then done

Quickly the skilled surgeon makes the initial incision

Not as the timorous biology student dissecting his first frog.…

I need not ask forgiveness for these thoughts because you know me

And understand the inferiority that surrounds and enfolds me.

So quickly then … Do you cut…?

Do you love?

Big Daddy Takes a Walk

Big Daddy swung down the street with his fingers snapping. He was there, all the way in orbit! Man! What a crazy scene! Everything was his way, there were no troubles. The cars on the street were brighter and the people's coats were cleaner. Nothing was bad. Everything was good. Big Daddy was high. Flying way high! He saw the fuzz two blocks ahead. No one who wasn't high would have noticed, but Big Daddy noticed. He knew he had to be real sharp to pierce his way through the thickening crowd of squares that milled about going to their jobs, whose dull mundane jobs that netted them only a small sense of security. What was really secure these days? Anything could happen!

Big Daddy had only one primary worry: the attorneys. Man, like they can be real tough! They were going to take Big Daddy to the cleaners! There wasn't too much he could do about it. Once a woman—or should he really qualify her as that—had made up her mind, there was no telling what the counselors could do. They could make Big Daddy scream for mercy if they wanted to. Big Daddy wasn't going to cry, though. He had had tougher battles! Why, remember when he had been chased for speeding and evading arrest? And what about the time Jimmy was going to dust him? Man, these law men were nothing to Big Daddy! Man, he would show them! He would tell them plenty! There was still justice, you know. They couldn't penalize him more than he made, could they? Of course not! He would give her just so much and that is all. No more. No less.

As he swaggered down the street, he argued his case. What time was he due in court? 9:45 a.m. … plenty of time for a cup of coffee. These dumb broads were no match for Big Daddy! He would show them! Just wait until he got through questioning her! She would really squirm just like all the squares squirm when the pressure got rough. 9:30 … just fifteen minutes till court. Boy, he could hardly wait to get there. It would take him five minutes to walk over to the courthouse; five minutes to move from the doorway to the escalator; off the escalator down the long corridor to the judges chambers; one minute to identify himself and walk into the room of reckoning. He could hardly wait. He finished his coffee. While paying his check, he lit a cigarette and swung from the drugstore with fingers snapping once again.

He moved through the dull crowds with obvious alacrity. Man, in just thirty minutes, he would have her begging to take him back! Let's see now, on which floor is the judge holding the hearing? Well, he'll find out at the information desk. He stepped up his tempo and stride as he checked his watch for the correct time. 6 minutes to go. Man, the nerve of that broad to sue him for divorce and ask all that crazy loot for two lousy kids. Man, he was really going to let her have it! 4 minutes to go, as he saw the building loom into view. Man, it was a buggy looking spot, all soot stained, tired, gray and ominous. 2 minutes to go, as he pushed the door inward and walked to the desk. Like, man, was he going to tell her a few things! She was anything but from hipsville. A real nothing! You can't con this cool cat. I'll cool her in a hurry. He smiled at the girl back of the desk as he asked, "How much is a one way trip to Pittsburgh?"

Note: A bitter divorce in 1960 prompted Gordon to write the story, "Big Daddy."

The Lady of St. Regis

I pulled my sedan into the parking space easily. After driving this particular piece, 20,000 miles in the past three months, I knew the car as well as I knew my own body. After locking the doors, I looked for Brown and Latham. They were right behind me when I found my place, then I saw them a half block up on the right.

While I wait for them, let me introduce myself. I am George Sholes, 29 years old, married, but not quite, five feet nine, 170 pounds, well-tanned, not because of athletics but because of my line of work. I give a false impression of being a very muscular person and very athletic, as I wear the right clothes to create this impression. I have a crew cut, or butch, whatever you wish to call it.

"Man, I sure hope we find some decent-looking broads in here," remarked Brown, a little heatedly. We had just knocked him out of the saddle a few minutes beforehand and he was still a little angry. "Quit worrying, that gal was old enough to be your mother; and on top of that, the way she was built, I don't think anyone could get too excited." "What do you mean … she was a woman, wasn't she?" That was obviously the wrong thing to say. Both Latham and I said, "Prove it." Brown laughed. "Okay, okay, let's see if everything they say about the St. Regis is true."

We walked toward the St. Regis, a spot recommended by several of the local people we met on the show as being a good spot to pick up a little tail. As we walked in, I told Latham and Brown to go ahead, get a table and that I would be along in a minute. I left them and went over to the bar. I sat down on the high stool and ordered the usual for me, CC and water.

The fellow next to me finished his drink and left. That left one empty stool the entire length of the long bar. A tall, slim chap started to sit down next to me when the bartender strode up and said, "I'm sorry, sir, but that seat is taken." "By whom?" asked the fellow. "By that young lady right there, sir," said the bartender.

I turned slightly and thought, "they sure move fast in here." I haven't even started on this drink and already they are getting me lined up. The young lady he referred to sat down next to me. I tried not to appear obvious as I looked her over. About 27, probably five feet four, dark-brown hair, the kind of features that would one day be heavy, but now were just right.

She had blue eyes as I was to discover later. A well-proportioned girl and she had a very clean wholesome look about her.

The minute she sat down, the bartender fixed her a drink and they began what appeared to be a serious conversation. I naturally assumed it concerned me and what I would be charged, etc. The bartender left to fill an order and I turned to her and said, "Are you a working girl?" "Yes," she said. Graciously, I asked her, "May I buy you a drink?" She accepted saying, "Thank you." I ordered two more. She was drinking rum and Coke, so I had another CC and water. I asked, "How much?" She looked at her drink saying, "$25.00." I responded, "Enjoy your drink." I wasn't going to pay any broad $25.00. Sounding rather disgusted she said, "Thanks, I will." She was a little angry. Apparently she thought she had an easy one. Well, I wasn't. Frankly, I'm not used to paying for it. I have always been lucky with women. Don't ask me why, but I always seem to make out well.

I expected her to get up and leave now that she knew I was not going to be a mark. Instead she and the bartender continued their conversation. She kept glancing across the bar to the alcove that led to the rest rooms. Two men were standing there surveying the scene. The hair on the back of my neck prickled just a little. I don't care—if you're in this business, you sense the law. Then some of the pictures began to make sense. I turned to her again but this time very obviously and said, "Look, are you in trouble?" She looked surprised and answered with, "How did you know?" "Well," I said. "I noticed the two men over in the alcove and I figured they might be closing in. Am I right?" Looking frightened, she looked at me and said, "I think so. There has been big trouble upstairs and the fuzz has been brought in. I'm scared and I've never been picked up and I don't want to be." I told her, "Alright look, let me go to the men's room. I'll be right back and then we'll get out of here." Adamantly, she responded with, "No. No! That won't do. The minute I leave they'll nab me." I turned and looked at her saying, "No, they won't. You have to be caught in the act and we won't let that happen. Look, just sit here. I'll be right back."

I slid off the stool and walked to the alcove. I sized them up as I went by. They were the fuzz alright. NO mistaking them! I went on into the rest room and wondered if she would still be there when I got back. She was. We finished our drinks, got off our bar stools and walked out as inconspicuously as possible. I had no chance to tell Latham or Brown that I was leaving. Oh well, they'll be alright. We walked along for a minute.

Then she started to look back. "Can it," I hissed. Continuing I said, "Don't do anything to make them suspicious. We haven't done a thing wrong, so quit worrying." By this time, sex had left me, and the excitement of what was happening had taken over. I helped her into the car and then I joined her. I eased the sedan out of the parking place and headed down the street. "You are going to have to direct me," I told her. "Just keep going straight for about three blocks and then turn left," she said with accuracy. "Look, just in case they should stop us, my name is George Sholes. What's yours?" Looking around behind her, timidly she said, "Pat, Pat Braden."

Note: (When Gordon was 29, he was married, but not quite, five feet nine, 170 pounds, and well-tanned with crew cut hair.)

CHAPTER THREE
The Merger: Television and Wrestling

One Good Try

Each day you learn a little.
Why doubt?
Why say this will pass over and you will forget this?
Like all else ... keep your confidence ... keep the exuberance....
Keep the fire and the compulsion.
You have made half attempts at living for thirty years
Now at least make one good honest try.
Give it everything you've got ... at least when and if you fail you'll know
You gave it everything you had ... and when and if you
Accomplish what you want ... it will be a contest well won.

From the Gordon Solie Collection

Chief Little Eagle, above left, spoke with Gordon during the infancy of "Cowboy" Luttrall's *Championship Wrestling from Florida* (*CWF*). In 1959, Gordon and friend Milt Spencer filled the hosts' chairs when the studio shows appeared on WFLA-Channel 8. Gordon continued announcing on television with *Championship Wrestling from Florida* until August of 1987. One of his many broadcasting accomplishments included remaining a host of this popular television show for 27 consecutive years.

From the Gordon Solie Collection

Chicago's nationally known wrestling promoter, Bob Luce (above left), gave an interview with Gordon in January of 1962. The clarity of the picture is poor, as it is a photograph taken of an old television set tuned into *Championship Wrestling from Florida*.

From the Gordon Solie Collection

The "Assassins," above left and right, posed before their next studio tag-team match. From left to right above; Tom Renesto, manager "The Good Doctor" and Jody Hamilton.

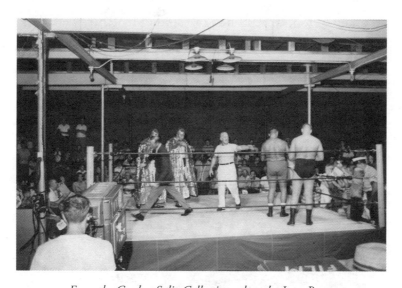

From the Gordon Solie Collection: photo by Jerry Prater

Gordon was hurrying out of the ring in the picture above after announcing the wrestlers for the next event. Referee Johnny Carlin signaled the wrestlers to rap up the autograph session so the tag-team match could begin.

From the Gordon Solie Collection: photo by Jerry Prater

Gordon (above back) prepared to interview the "Assassins" at the studio for a show aired on Channel 13 (WTVT). Below, the "Assassins" joined Gordon after completing a tag-team match. This was about 1963, when the TV studio matches were first filmed at the Sportatorium in Tampa, Fla.

From the Gordon Solie Collection: photo by Jerry Prater

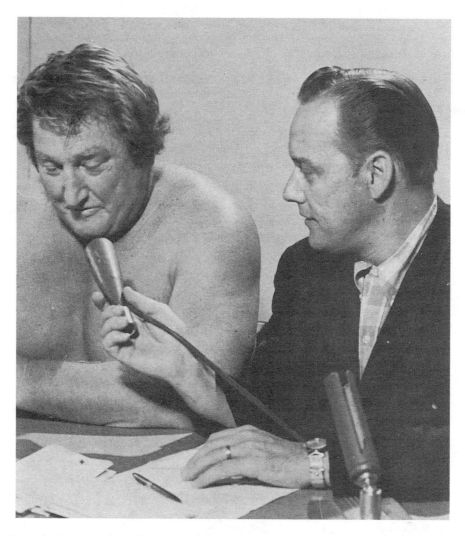

From the Gordon Solie Collection: photo from the files of Ross Parsons © by Rogo Corporation

Wrestler "Yukon" Eric (Eric Holmbach) shared the mike with Gordon in the early 1960s. Personal misfortunes led to Eric's suicide in 1965. He is remembered fondly by many, including the SLAM Wrestling Canadian Hall of Fame.

Sirens of Life

The wail of the siren is an apt description
It's the sound of the professional mourner in advance

Sonny Myers, pictured below, spoke about meeting Gordon in Florida, "I was impressed with Gordon. He took the time to stop and listen to people. Gordon didn't give the fans a lot of bull. He explained to the fans the type of holds the wrestlers were performing or attempting to execute. He was the best."

When asked about his favorite title Sonny replied, "That would be the first title I won in front of my home town fans in St. Josephs, Miss. It was the Missouri Heavyweight Championship."

From the Gordon Solie Collection

From the Gordon Solie Collection

Don Eagle, a member of the Mohawk Tribe of Canada, was popular with viewers during the early years of televised wrestling. Tampa wrestling fans saw Don at live events as well, including a match against World Champion "Killer" Kowalski in March of 1960 at Fort Homer Hesterly Armory.

From the Gordon Solie Collection

Judy Glover battled the likes of Ella Waldek and Millie Stafford for the Women's Southern Championship in 1957. When Gordon initiated fan clubs for professional wrestlers in Tampa, Judy's followers immediately started one for her.

From the Gordon Solie Collection

An early picture of Frankie Cain, who became known to wrestling fans as one of the masked "Infernos" and also as the "Great Mephisto." Frankie, a boxer before his wrestling days, met Gordon in 1950 while Gordon worked for WEBK Radio. They had more in common than just sports; they both liked a watering hole named Guys and Dolls near the bridge in downtown Tampa. Nine years later, when "Cowboy" Luttrall aired his first wrestling program on WFLA-TV, the first match paired Frankie against Ray Villmer.

From the Gordon Solie Collection

Gordon praised the athletic ability of the "Fabulous Moolah" (Lillian Ellison), and her dominance of women's professional wrestling. Rocky Marciano showed his supremacy as a professional heavyweight boxer with a record of 49 consecutive wins and no losses.

From the Gordon Solie Collection

This was not the hold that wrestling fans expected to be put onto the "Sheik" (Ed Farhat). *Sports Shots with Solie* read as follows on March 1, 1960: "I have seen everything now; I have seen wrestlers use almost every conceivable device or weapon in order to win a match, but I have never seen anything quite as spectacular as a man who spurts fire from his fingertips. Several fans gave me theories as to how it was accomplished last week when the 'Sheik' suddenly blinded and stunned 'Irish' Danny McShain with a burst of fire during their bout. I saw it happen and still can't figure it out. I asked the 'Sheik' about this during the week, and received no answer that is printable. Well, maybe the answer will be found one day. As yet, there is no rule forbidding the use of fire, so it remains a legal enigma in wrestling."

From the Gordon Solie Collection: photo by Jerry Prater

Lou Thesz, six-time National Wrestling Alliance World Heavyweight Champion (above right), applied a flying dropkick to his opponent.

The Resilient Man

The resiliency of man
Becomes ever increasing
As he grows younger in thought.
It is mental age that
Breaks man and shatters
His physical shell.
In changing thought there is youth
In sedentary thinking there is eventual ruin.

In late 1959, the Southern Wrestling Alliance met in Atlanta, Ga., to revise rules, plan a pictorial revue of the wrestlers, unify the Alliance members, and crack down on unscrupulous promoters.

Gordon drew his ideas of possible cover seals for the proposed 1960 Southern Wrestling Alliance book. His first sketch emphasized the strength of the Southern States working together.

From the Gordon Solie Collection

From the Gordon Solie Collection

Bonnie Watson (below) won the Southern Women's Title in 1960 and the Florida Women's Championship in 1971. She married the charming gentleman, referee Stu Schwartz.

From the Gordon Solie Collection

From the Gordon Solie Collection

Mike Paidousis of Knoxville, Tenn., captured the Central States Heavyweight Title in September of 1960.

From the Gordon Solie Collection

Reggie Parks (above left) and Don Curtis were partnered up in a tag-team match. Don went on to win the World Tag Team Championship with Mark Lewin in 1963 and again with Abe Jacobs in 1964. Below, Don reached to tag Reggie while maintaining control of Roy Heffernan.

From the Gordon Solie Collection

Something Left Behind

Some of the most memorable junior heavyweight action ever in professional wrestling took place when Hiro Matsuda (below right) climbed into the ring with Danny Hodge (below left). Referee Charlie Laye looked on as the two men began to grapple. As an amateur wrestler, Hodge won three NCAA championships at the University of Oklahoma. The matches between these two competitors were some of Gordon's favorites.

From the Gordon Solie Collection: photo by Jerry Prater

The Texas Women's title changed hands twice in 1963 between the ladies in the next two photographs.

SWEET GEORGIA BROWN
Girl Wrestler----Columbia, South Carolina

From the Gordon Solie Collection

BETTY ANN SPENCER
Girl Wrestler........Atlanta, Georgia

From the Gordon Solie Collection

Frankie Cain remembers working the wrestling circuit with Tim Woods and driving through 1960s Southern states like Louisiana. They were not well received when they stopped for food breaks, because people saw two white men in a car with two black women in the back seat. The ladies traveling with them to the next wrestling card were Betty Ann Spencer and Sweet Georgia Brown.

From the Gordon Solie Collection

Eddie Graham (pictured above) signed autographs for fans before a 1964 boxing match. Don Curtis (below right) escorted Eddie away from the squared circle following the bout.

From the Gordon Solie Collection

Something Left Behind

From the Gordon Solie Collection

After his boxing match, Eddie Graham (above right) laughed it up a little with Don Curtis in the locker room.

Courtesy of The Tampa Tribune: staff photo by Dan Fager

Gordon's face was not only recognizable to wrestling TV viewers by 1964, but his image also was associated with stock car racing and charity. Above, Gordon showed a putter, which was a door prize for the Babe Zaharias Cancer Memorial Fund Dinner. Some of Gordon's charitable contributions over the years included:

Police Athletic League, publicity; Florida Sheriff's Association, honorary lifetime member (Sheriff's Boys Ranch); Babe Zaharias Sports Week, chairman; American Cancer Society, Hillsborough County, board member; Muscular Dystrophy, emcee for telethon; Division of Youth Services, volunteer; MISD (Muscular Injuries and Skeletal Disease), board member; Tampa Bay Buccaneers and Pro wrestlers' charity softball, voice of the wrestlers; Leukemia Society of America, Suncoast Chapter, board member; NCAA Soccer National Championship, volunteer; United Cerebral Palsy, volunteer; Big Brothers/Big Sisters of Tampa Bay, volunteer; SERVE (School Enrichment Resource Volunteers in Education Honors), volunteer; and Florida Child's Wish Come True, Inc., board member.

Referee Stu Schwartz looked on below as Eddie Graham attempted to arm whip Gene Kiniski across the ring. Kiniski took over the NWA World Heavyweight title in 1966.

From the Gordon Solie Collection: photo by Jerry Prater

Louis Tillet (below left) and Eduardo Perez (below right) had "Sputnik" Monroe in a bad way on the turnbuckle.

From the Gordon Solie Collection: photo by Jerry Prater

Self-Menagerie

Man must justify
This is true
Yet so many refuse to deny
Ours is not a small scope to see
But a broad encompassing menagerie
Each little animal struggling to exist
With no thought of his brother save to subsist
We call on our gods for wisdom and truth
Yet we ourselves stay locked in a booth
Slide open the doors, step out in the light
And then my friend, offer the fight

From the Gordon Solie Collection: photo by Jerry Prater

Les Welch (above right) was the first Florida Heavyweight Champion to be recognized as such by the National Wrestling Alliance (NWA).

From the Gordon Solie Collection

Bette Boucher won the NWA Women's World title in a 1966 Seattle match.

From the Gordon Solie Collection

Ron Reed became more familiar to wrestling fans as the blond-haired "Buddy Colt."

From the Gordon Solie Collection

Two of the top National Wrestling Alliance (NWA) promoters of the age, Sam Muchnick (above left, St. Louis booking office) and Paul Jones (above right, Atlanta booking office), were looking at pictures of the "Assassins" in 1968. Below, Jack Welch scowled as he twisted the left arm of the "Great" Malenko.

From the Gordon Solie Collection

The agile Cyclon Negro, on his hands in the picture below, took over the Florida Heavyweight Title in 1969.

From the Gordon Solie Collection: photo by Jerry Prater

From the Gordon Solie Collection

Chati Yokouchi (above) united with Mr. Ito in 1969 to claim the Georgia Tag Team Championship. Later, Yokouchi teamed with Yasa Fuji to win the North American Tag Team belts at Memorial Hall in Kansas City, Kan., (1972).

From the Gordon Solie Collection

Jack Brisco pulled a back-heel trip on Ray Stevens.

Sunday Morning

Flies on the bar

Muscled young men in and around the pool

A mildly attractive woman … naked in her physical interest.

Rusting storage doors spoil the image of opulence.

And so she sat to watch the show

CHAPTER FOUR
Lessons

Power Buttons

The sun glinted sharply and returned to the heavens, reflecting from the aluminum surface of the four engine jet transport circling the field at Washington. The pilot patiently awaited final approach instructions from the tower. The earphones crackled and he made a somewhat hurried reply. Several tons of metal then changed course making a dog leg to the right and lowered its landing gear.

The pilot tensed somewhat as he watched the ground approach. He waited for the first slight bump and the high bark of spinning wheels coming in contact with the concrete surface of the air strip … the bark, the blending of burning rubber with the uncountable black strips already on the well-used landing surface. The plane was down. A small sigh escaped the pilot as he taxied the plane. It was good to be back in Washington. He knew the Chief felt that way, too. The Chief was back in the plush section of the airliner, getting set—he felt sure—to meet the many dignitaries who would be on hand. The Chief was preparing himself for the press, newsreels and the Vice President's greeting.

The plane swung around easily and stopped. The whining jets slowly died away. The pilot opened the door of the passenger compartment greeted by the now-famous wide-open, friendly smile. This smile was known the world around as the harbinger of peace to people everywhere. "Whenever you're ready, Sir." "In a moment, I want to make sure this briefcase is properly locked again," the Chief responded. The pilot smiled. He didn't know what was in the case, but the Chief seemed very concerned with it. "I think we are ready now. Open the door," announced the Chief.

The sounds of the world came rushing into the plane as the door swung open. Secret Service men were standing by the steps leading down to the ground. The Vice President was the first in line of many dignitaries and members of the press, radio, television and newsreels. The Vice President greeted him warmly, "Nice to have you back in Washington again, sir." "Very good to be back," was the reply. "Your car is the second in line, but I assume you will want to speak to the press first." "Yes, I will be glad to answer their questions."

The press closed in eagerly, microphones were turned on and the cameras began to whir. Somebody asked, "How does it feel to be back in Washington?" The reply was the obvious, "Very good. Very good, indeed." Then followed the usual barrage of questions: some kind, some sharp, all curious. Moments later he strode to the long black limousine that was waiting for him with several aides from the House. They entered and the car pulled smoothly out into the streets of Washington.

—

At the Pentagon, two secretaries were checking their makeup in the powder room. They were preparing to leave their respective offices for the day to enjoy a quick cocktail before going to their apartments for a light dinner. "I wonder what the purpose of his visit really is," remarked the blonde. "I don't know, nor do I really care," retorted her co-worker. Continuing, she said, "All I know is that he sure has caused me a lot of extra work. My boss is working late again tonight, another conference with the other brass over his visit." "Well, he stopped by our office the last time and he certainly was nice," the blonde said in a defensive tone. "Frankly, I think he is the nicest one that has ever been here." Her co-worker came back with, "How would you know? He's the only one you've ever seen or known." "You're right, of course," said the blonde, "but everybody seems to like him." In agreement, her co-worker added, "Well, he is the most popular man in the country today, that's for sure."

He was being discussed in other circles, too. The Chiefs of Staff were gathered around the large conference table. One could tell there was more than a little consternation regarding the visit. The head of the Space Agency appeared the most worried of the group seated around the table. "I tell you they are still at least five years ahead of us." "Well, that might be right," replied the Air Force, "but remember that we can still strike back quickly and effectively and—" "And don't forget we now have fifteen atomic subs equipped with atomic missiles," interrupted the Navy, "plus the fact our artillery is now completely atomically equipped and our ground forces are in constant readiness." "You've got to remember," continued the Army, "we now have the most modern and efficient radar system in existence today. We will believe this time!" He concluded confidently, "There will never be another Pearl Harbor!"

—

The car continued toward the center of Washington. The Premier leaned back against the upholstery and relaxed for the first time in many hours. His aides plied him with several questions about home, the trip and the weather. Everyone was careful to conceal their eagerness and curiosity about the rumored purpose for the Premier's visit.

—

Special Agent Bill Colwell of the Secret Service left the airport and went immediately to the office of his superior, Captain Ed Simpson. "Nothing unusual, Captain," was his opening comment. "He arrived on schedule, dressed in a dark blue suit, white shirt, dark blue tie with small white stripes, black socks and black shoes. He carried his usual briefcase, was very cordial and, of course, he smiled." Simpson grunted, "Well, I guess you were thorough enough … nothing unusual though, eh?" "No sir." "What do you think, Colwell? Why do you think he is here this time?" Colwell pondered the question answering, "I wish I knew, sir. I wish I could put my finger on it. There was something too gracious about him, almost too eager to talk, like he was bubbling over with some new secret. I wish I knew." "Well," the Captain said, "send the usual squad over to cover, you know, just like before." "O.K., O.K., Captain." Colwell got up, started to leave, suddenly stopped, and turned around. "Captain?" "Yes." "How about letting me kind of hang around for the duration of his stay?" "Don't you think you are a little over anxious about this Colwell?" "O.K., O.K," said Simpson. "You are a free agent while he is here. Let me know if anything interesting turns up, like what time he bathes Saturday, huh?" "Sure Captain, anything you say." Colwell left still bothered.

The phone rang at the White House. The call was shunted immediately to the Chief Executive's office. "Mr. President?" "Yes?" "Everything went off very smoothly. He arrived on schedule, seemed to be in very good spirits and sent his regards and greetings." "Fine, fine." The reply was hearty from the Chief of State. "Glad to hear it. Give my best to your wife and family. I will see you in the morning as planned." "Very good, sir, see you in the morning." "Oh, by the way," asked the President. "Yes?" "Any indication as to why he is here?" "None, sir." Across the nation that night and the next morning, radios, television and the newspapers carried stories and pictures of the Premier's arrival in the United States.

—

Professor W. Bryan Wibbs, Associate Professor of Biology at Central College, read the article with usual calm. An unhurried man, Wibbs had complete faith in the indestructibility of life and consequences. His outlook on life was one of serenity and composure. He casually remarked to his wife over his second cup of coffee that he was taking over Professor Wolfe's class today on bacteriology. This was done as a prelude to a conversation he wanted to have with her regarding his latest research work. His wife, a pretty, clear-featured girl, looked up expectantly when he spoke and followed his lead in the conversation.

Several hours later, Professor Wibbs entered the classroom where Wolfe's students waited. For some reason, his mind drifted back to the article and the picture of the Premier's smiling face. He quickly dismissed it again, setting his mind on the more important tasks at hand. His concluding comments on his lecture had a positive ring to them. "And so you see, no matter what happens with in the small scope of us and our neighbors ... life will continue. No matter what degree of heat or cold ever sets upon this planet, bacteria will live on and eventually emerge again. That is all for today. Professor Wolfe will be back tomorrow." The students left the lecture room with the exception of one tall, crewcut lad. The student's tone of voice reflected doubt as he asked, "Do you really believe that, Professor Wibbs?" "If I didn't, do you think I would waste my time lecturing on it?" was the quick rejoinder.

—

The Premier rose at his usual hour that same morning, roughly 5:30. He showered quickly using lukewarm water at first, following it up with cold. His body was still reasonably hard for a man of 63. He squinted slightly as he looked at the picture of himself in the mirror. Not an unhandsome face! A little florid, perhaps, from the last few years of softer living. He brushed his teeth using precise regular motions. They were still all his! He checked the medicine cabinet and found a can of instant lather. Bless the Americans for this, he thought to himself. In a matter of moments he was through and back in his room selecting his wardrobe for the day. Conservative but yet quite American ... that would fill the bill for today.

After dressing, he opened the door and went downstairs to the main dining room. His aides, the Ambassador, and all attachés were on hand waiting for him. They knew of his early waking habits and had set their alarms ahead considerably to be on hand, on time. His peasant's face broke into a smile, and he greeted them before they had a chance to make the usual salutations.

Breakfast consisted of the best Canadian bacon, extra-large eggs, Florida orange juice, toast and coffee. No one spoke during the breakfast except to ask for salt or sugar. On the second round of coffee, the Premier began to issue the orders for the day. First to the Ambassador; "Make arrangements to acquire the largest hall in Washington. Bring me the complete floor plan. Also, arrange for a tour for me to see the Pentagon, the State Department, Congress, etc. I will be glad to speak to Congress on an informal basis.

Remember, not a formal speech." The Ambassador did not question his orders. His only comment was to inquire as to when the Premier wanted the hall and for how long. "I will want the hall immediately. We will want to use it for two weeks."

To his chief aide he said, "Find the best printer in Washington. Hire him to stand by for the next four or five days to take an order for 3,000 invitations." If his aide was surprised he didn't show it, but looks of surprise crossed several normally stolid faces at the table.

"And now, gentlemen, I shall tell you what is going to happen." His smile grew very broad. "We are going to throw the largest, most lavish party ever seen in this country. It will equal anything you have ever read about in the days of Rome!" Scanning their faces, he issued more orders: "Igor, you will handle all the food arrangements; Joseph, the liquids; Peter, the music. The party is one week from today. No one shall miss the affair. I want every member of Congress, all Chiefs of Staff, all foreign Ambassadors. I want this to be the grandest, most successful party ever held in Washington. Is that clear?" The question amounted to an order.

Leaning over to the gentleman seated on his left, the Premier said, "Urislav, I wish to confer with you privately." The others at the table took their cues and left immediately. Urislav, a man of medium height and weight, waited for the Premier to speak. "Urislav, how many men do you have here in Washington at the present?" Promptly Urislav answered, "Only eleven here in Washington. I have four at Los Alamos, six at Cape Canaveral and three at Vandenberg in California." "Well," the Premier stated, "call them back immediately. Have them here by tomorrow morning."

—

The President cleared his throat and looked around the table to see if everyone was seated. The President, Secretary of State, the House Leaders, the Secretary of Defense, as well as the heads of the Armed Services were present. Satisfied that everyone was ready he began, "Gentlemen, no one knows why he is here. We have been unable to learn any concrete reason for his visit. Does anyone have anything to report?" No one answered. Acknowledging the lack of response, he continued, "I take it, then, we are just as much in the dark as we were last week. Does anyone have any theories that we haven't gone over yet? Or any conclusions left un-drawn?" Again, silence.

The voice of the Vice-President broke the lingering silence, "Do you possibly think that his goodwill touring and the soft policy they have affected could really be true?" A voice several seats down answered, "Yes, there is a merit to this idea. It could conceivably be that these people have realized that we are still the most powerful country in the world," stated the Secretary of State. "No, I don't think this new attitude means a thing! I think it is just another part of their master plan to rule the world and the universe!" said the Space Agency Secretary almost heatedly. "These men are ahead of us in almost everything." "Oh, come on now, Les," interrupted the Secretary of the Air Force, "you still have the Army and Navy and us, you know." Nodding as he answered, "I know we have, but unfortunately I don't think it is going to be good enough to combat a successful rocket campaign." "Well then, why don't you do something about it?" asked the Secretary of the Navy, decidedly heated now. "We are doing all we can but you can't catch up overnight!" Les retorted bitterly. "What with limited budgets and all…."

The tones of the words were becoming hot and politely offensive. "Now, now, gentlemen, there is no point in getting too excited. For all we know he might just like it better here than over there," the Vice President slid in humorously, waiting for a sign of humor. "That's exactly what worries me," Les replied with a little rancor in voice. His thoughts drifted back momentarily to last week when he asked for another 2 billion dollars for rocket research, and the leaders in Congress along with the Heads of State had refused. Their answer was simple. The Navy and Air Force needed more planes—jet planes. The leader of the Liberal Party spoke up at this point. "Mr. President, as the leader of my party, I feel it is my right to speak quite plainly about this matter. I feel too much emphasis is being placed on the mere fact that a Head of State of a foreign power is here in the United States. We feel there are many other pressing matters to attend to. You know there is an election in just 16 months. Many of us have a lot of campaigning to do if we want to return to Washington next year." Not to be left out, the Conservative Party spoke next, "As much as I hate to agree with my esteemed colleague," he said this smilingly, "I, too, believe we are putting too much emphasis on this matter. Surely his visit here will not create any earth-shattering events."

"Perhaps you're right," the President agreed. "Perhaps we are making a mountain out of a molehill. If no one has anything more to say, I guess we can adjourn." Glances were exchanged, by silent mutual assent; they waited perhaps 30 seconds and then rose to leave, each with his mind full of personal problems.

Bill Colwell had personal problems, too. His sinuses were bothering him again. He debated whether or not to go to the doctors again and finally decided against it. He wanted to check with the men who were at the Embassy House keeping it under surveillance.

He dialed Dan Johnson's number and waited while the rings finally roused the now-sleeping Dan.

When Dan answered the phone, there was no need for Colwell to identify himself. Colwell simply inquired, "Anything happen last night?" Johnson's immediate response was a stifled yawn followed by a voice of slight irritation saying, "Hell, no, I would have called! You know that." Colwell apologetically said, "Yeah, I'm sorry I bothered you. Go on back to bed." Well, maybe the men would have more to report.

The day men could add nothing of consequence. Hours rolled into days and nights and finally Washington began to buzz with rumors of the party. Word leaked from the printers, the liquor distributors and the rental agency. Soon it was verified by the White House news agency that the Premier was holding a very special party. It was assumed that this party must have some political significance because of the unusual guest list and the number invited.

The Premier, meanwhile, held several conferences with Urislav, both men studying the floor plans of the large reception hall. Entrances and exits were studied with extreme scrutiny. "Place our butlers at each entrance and exit, Urislav. I will give them their instructions at three o'clock the afternoon of the party." "Yes, Sir." Urislav's dark eyes held a slight question that did not go unnoticed by the Premier. No answers now, he thought, no answers yet….

The invitations were worded in such a way as to preclude anyone's refusal for any reason barring health. Transatlantic cables carried coded messages back and forth regarding the oddly worded invitations. Heads of State pondered the forthcoming event with studied concentration.

At three o'clock on the afternoon of the affair, the Premier walked into the room where the butlers waited for instructions. Ten minutes later, the Premier left. With the exception of a few last-minute details that only the Premier could handle, everything was in readiness.

That evening, the Premier ate somewhat sparingly. A glass of bicarbonate followed. He belched mildly. This was the only indication that he was even slightly nervous about the forthcoming festivities. At 8 p.m., he began to dress, choosing carefully everything he was going to wear. 8:30 p.m. found him ready and now checking the small brown briefcase he carried with him from the plane. At 8:45 p.m., he went to the radio room. The operator was startled to see him. "Yes, Sir?" "Contact my office immediately." "Yes, Sir," she answered. The operator came alive working the maze of dials that brought direct communication with the Premier's office in the homeland. The Premier handed the operator a message in a new code.

Six minutes later, contact was made. The message was sent. The answer received. The Premier smiled grimly. Everything was ready. He strode out of the room down the hall to a door, out into the night air to the waiting limousine. "To the party," he said gaily.

At 9:07 p.m. the Premier strode briskly into the rented hall. Urislav met him quickly. "Everyone is here except the ambassadors from Brazil, Ireland, Paraguay and Formosa," Urislav informed him. With a slight smile of satisfaction, the Premier said, "Small matter, enough are here, and we have exactly six minutes before I make my little speech for the night."

Six minutes later, the Premier mounted the stage area and stood behind the podium. He cleared his throat twice. Then he spoke in English. "Ladies and Gentlemen, may I have your attention for a moment please?" As if by magic, the immense hall was silent. This was most unusual. Everyone stood in amazed silence. They barely noticed the doors of the hall had been closed.

While the assembled stood amazed and silent, the Premier noted quickly that everyone was in place. "Now in order to avoid hysteria," the Premier began, "please listen closely to what I am going to say. To move or to cry out until I am finished will be pointless. Please note that each and every door is covered. As you would say in America, by two armed men, you are virtually my prisoners at the moment. I can assure you that in a few minutes you shall have your freedom. For decades now, our way of life has been opposed to yours. We, of our nation, believe firmly in the theory that the best-trained minds will rule the world. We have worked unceasingly toward that goal. Now we feel that we have reached the point where we are ready to put our theory in action. I am being very brief and to the point because simply, my friends, we do not have much time. In short, I am here to accept, in the name of our government, complete capitulation by all of the other governments."

A murmur rose from the gathering like the tide rolling into the beach, and like the tide, it faded when the Premier resumed speaking. As he spoke, he reached into the briefcase and pulled out a small black box affair. There were four large, white depressible buttons and one red button. "Gentlemen, I hold before you the key to the world. Each of these white buttons represents 20 key cities the world over. This red button represents every major military installation in the world. By merely depressing any one of the buttons, I will be responsible for the death of some 20 million people, all of you, myself included. At this moment, one million scientists and technicians are standing by, ready at my signal to fire all existing rockets in our homeland. There will be no chance for retaliation. There will be no chance for survival.

Gentlemen it is now 9:22 p.m. You have until 9:45 p.m. to give me an answer. That is only a few moments away. One foolish move or mistake and I will simply push these buttons, and then there will be no further mistakes."

The President's mind had been racing ahead of the Premier's for the past two minutes, desperately trying to figure how many chances for error would exist in rocketry. How many bases might be missed? How much retaliation might we be able to effect? It seemed as though every eye in the building was fixed directly on the President.

(The above was the beginning of a screen play written by Gordon.)

From the Gordon Solie Collection

The "Assassins" maintained the mystique of the mask while dressed in street clothes.

Picayune, Mississippi

A reminder ... write of Mack Parker

Coroner's jury ... he died from two high speed rifle bullets

By unknown terrorists

The Birds

They do not know dissent

They have never made a protest march

They know total and complete despair

They watch their young unborn

Not understanding why

They diminish with no realization

Understanding is not possible

We in our great depth have failed in the shallows

For them death will be gradual, peaceful

Ours ... as we deserve it

CHAPTER FIVE

Acceptance

Flying in '64

Twenty-six years and one month after the Wright brothers made their historic flight at Kitty Hawk, I entered this world on a frigid night in Minneapolis, Minnesota. As I grew up, much of my reading was about the air heroes of World War One. To me, these were the men who had the extra dash of glamour and excitement. My uncle Arthur, (who I never met), was killed in the battle of St. Mihiel outside of Thiacourt, France, during the final days of the first big war, and being so young it was impossible for me to relate to the real horrors of armed conflict.

My off days were filled with Cowboys and Indians and six shooter cap pistols, of model airplanes, handmade from kits of balsa wood, paper and airplane glue and the desire to be another Rickenbacher, Raoul Lufberry or a Richthofen.

Then came 1941, and America was sent spinning into another war to end all wars. Suddenly, I had a new set of heroes, Richard Bong and Joe Foss. I still wanted to share the excitement of being in charge of a machine that could defy earthly forces, propel me into the air and perform power dives, loops, figure eights and all the other maneuvers I read about so avidly before Pearl Harbor.

World War Two ended before I reached service age. Although I tried enlisting when I was sixteen, I was discovered and sent home, embarrassed that I could not serve when most of my older friends had already either been drafted or had volunteered. I particularly remember Keith, a neighbor's son, who was three years older than me when he enlisted in the Air Force and lasted 18 seconds in combat as a tail gunner on a B-17. He died over France.

I finally got my wish to join the Army Air Force on May 29, 1947, my mother's birthday. I was sworn in and rapidly found out that I was not going to become a pilot. I did wind up with fighter planes as a communications specialist. I worked as a VHF Technician on P-51s (later changed to F-51). I was killed one morning during pre-flight for the fighters, but that's another story.

My desire to learn to fly languished as I struggled to survive in civilian life. But in the mid-'60s, several of the wrestlers began to become private pilots. Les Welch rapidly became a legend amongst the wrestlers because of his skill in flying in all forms of weather. When Les came to Florida to compete, he also introduced charter flights to the Florida office, and it wasn't long before Eddie Graham got the bug to fly. Eddie, who was legally blind in one eye, quickly mastered the courses and became extremely proficient. The urge to fly became infectious and then Don Curtis, Danny Hodge, Sam Steamboat and Sam's wife, Laura, started taking lessons at the private side of Tampa International Airport.

I was into my sixth year of doing Championship Wrestling from Florida and by now had garnered the trust and friendship of the "boys." Don and Sam both kidded me that I should learn to fly. I passed it off until it became a challenge as Danny, with his sense of humor, sort of intimated that maybe it would be too tough for me. The others sort of joined in the ribbing and so I devised a plan; a rib on these guys who loved practical jokes. I had a mission that I outlined to my wife, Smoky, who had to become an integral part of the plan. We set about implementing our scheme which was going to set up the foursome for a great practical joke, but would pay for my flying lessons as well.

A standard practice in learning to fly is an exercise called touch-and-go landings. I decided that I would start taking flying lessons and progress to the point that I would become proficient in that phase of flying. Once I had gained enough experience, I planned to get each of my buddies to take me up flying and ask them while flying near the St. Petersburg Airport about that touch-and-go thing that pilots do. I knew that their pride would immediately press them to offer to demonstrate their skill! When they demonstrated the maneuver, I would remark, "Well, that doesn't look too tough to me."

After baiting them in to a discussion about touch-and-go landings, I planned to finally say, "Hell, I could do that with no sweat the next time around!" Naturally, they would disagree. Then I would offer to bet $100 that I could do it right then and there. I had figured that my flying lessons would cost about $400 to solo, and there were four of them, so a bet with each of them would pay for my lessons.

To put the plan in place, I went to the airport and signed up to take lessons. But I had to swear the instructor to absolute secrecy and then find out their schedule so I wouldn't cross paths with them. I began my flying lessons at six a.m. to avoid running into them. Don,

Danny and Sam were wrestling every night so they would never be around that early in the morning. Everything worked out perfectly. After about 8 hours of instruction, my teacher Milton announced I was ready to solo. "Great! How about right now?" I said as we flew back from St. Pete, where we had fine-tuned touch-and-go landings at my request. Milton told me that he wanted to have the tires changed before I soloed, because they were getting pretty well worn and didn't want to run any risk on my solo flight. It was Saturday and he said Monday morning at 6 a.m. would be the time. Fine with me!

Little did I know that I was in the process of being swerved by Milt and my pigeons! I left the airport, drove home and told my wife that Monday was the time. Then I was going to spring my trap. Yeah, sure!

Sunday, as we often did, we called Don and Dotty Curtis about getting together for dinner. Surprisingly enough they seemed a little reluctant to get together saying that Danny Hodge, Sam Steamboat and Laura were coming over and they only had enough steaks for the five of them.

Well, I didn't want to pass up an opportunity to really set them up so I said, "No problem, we'll bring our own steaks." "O.K., see your around 3 p.m.," Curtis sort of hesitantly said. Smoky and I commented about the apparent reluctance of Don and Dotty to have us over. It was strange behavior, to say the least. Little did we know what was happening in the Curtis household! We went to the supermarket, picked up two steaks and proceeded out to the lakeside home where Don and Dotty lived. Sam and Laura Steamboat were on hand as well as Danny Hodge. Now mind you, they had all just soloed so I figured I could find out some valuable information by feigning a great deal of interest in their progress. Boy, did I find out things!!!

During conversations with them, Laura suddenly said that the solo flight had been fun until the smoke bomb went off in the engine compartment as she was circling the field to land. Now, I must admit that was a bit unnerving. I pressed on with more questions and when we had finished dinner, Smoke and I headed back home. In the car, I turned to her and said, "Well, we got them, they don't suspect a thing." My wife agreed whole-heartedly. I turned in early that night so I would be totally fresh in the morning for my solo flight. I was strung out like a two-pound test line trying to hold a 12-pound bass.

The next morning I arrived at the airport and my instructor Milt was waiting. We did a preflight on the aircraft, cranked her up, taxied out, got permission from the tower and took off, flying directly to St. Petersburg Airport. Five minutes later we landed and taxied to a location next to the terminal. Milt got out, gave me last-minute instructions and told me to go take off, request a left turn out and fly a landing pattern back to the field. I did as I was told and will admit my landing was probably the best I have ever made. Wow, the exultation when that plane left the ground. Here I was alone and being in charge of the plane was beyond belief, unless you've been there! It was, indeed, a thrill of a lifetime! Much better than your first taste of sex!

While I was taxiing back to the terminal, the tower instructed me to park there and go to the tower to the meet the operators. I proceeded up to the tower, Milt introduced me to the operators, and they showed me around and began to give a brief lesson on the art of being a tower operator. I found this, too, a tad strange because none of my pigeons mentioned anything at all about a tour of the tower after they soloed.

Milt and I finally went back to the plane and took off for Tampa International, where I was going to drop Milt and then take back off, flying to the practice area to play a little. Upon leaving St. Petersburg, we radioed the Tampa tower for landing instructions. The Tampa tower came back with a very strange response, "Uh … 77 Yankee?" "Is Milt on board?" Milt took the mike and responded, "10-4 Tampa tower, this is Milt, go ahead…." "Ahh … 77 Yankee … there is a code 13 in existence at the moment." "Roger, Tampa tower. What do you suggest?" Milt queried. "77 Yankee, proceed to practice area and maintain your current altitude until we get back to you." Naturally, I asked Milt what was going on and his answer was a little vague. However, in my high state of excitement, I accepted his answer without question. About 10 minutes after the radio sprang back to life, "77 Yankee, this is Tampa tower." "Roger, Tampa tower, this is iced 77 Yankee." "77 Yankee, code 13 has been cleared. You may proceed back to the airport to land as originally scheduled." "Roger, Tampa tower." "Ah, 77 Yankee, report inbound five miles out for landing instructions." "Roger, Tampa tower," Milt responded. We landed without incident, although I was just a little sloppy at touchdown. We taxied to the private terminal and Milt instructed me to shut off the engine, and come into the terminal so he could sign off on my log book that I had soloed. Then I could go back up and practice if I wished. We exited the 182 Cessna and walked into the terminal, where, to my complete astonishment, I was met by Don and Dotty Curtis, Eddie and Lucy Graham, Sam and Laura Steamboat, Danny Hodge, and—of all people—my wife,

Smoky! There was a six-piece rock and roll band and Andy Hardy, a sports reporter for Channel 13, filming it all! Well, they clipped my shirt tail, pinned wings on me and the band played on.

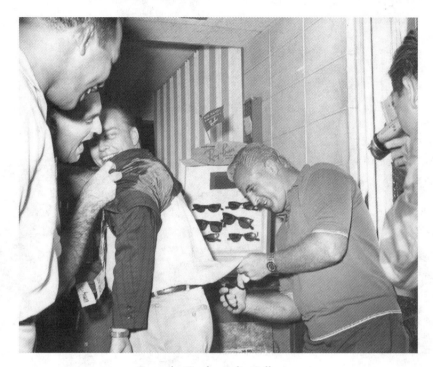

From the Gordon Solie Collection

Don Curtis held up Gordon's jacket while Eddie Graham performed the shirt cutting ceremony and Sam Steamboat egged them on.

From the Gordon Solie Collection

One of the pranksters, Don Curtis (above left), laughed heartily about the joke he and the gang played on Gordon.

I was caught, I had been had, and worst of all, I thought my wife had betrayed me. That was not the case however; it was Sam Steamboat who, on the morning that he was scheduled to make his first solo cross-country, spotted me at the terminal. When he returned to Tampa, he cornered Milt and managed to find out what I was up to.

Well, from that point on they knew more about my progress than I did. The delay in letting me solo was to allow them to make their final plans for the band, the wings and Andy Hardy to film it all. Oh yes, they also had a photographer on hand, as evidenced in the pages herein. When all was said and done, I had to take everyone out for breakfast. That set me back about 70 bucks and lots of embarrassment. I did find out over an "eat crow" that Smoky received a phone call at 6 a.m. from Dotty asking for me. Smoke, still half-asleep, responded that I was out flying; "uh … fryin … uh I don't know where he is…." Then Dotty told her what was happening and advised her to meet them at the airport private terminal. Eddie Graham said at breakfast, "Gordon, never try to fool the pros." A lesson I never forgot. The swerver had become the swervee.

In one sense, it was the turning point in my career in wrestling, because I suddenly realized that I had to rank as "one of the boys" to have them go to those lengths to reverse a rib in that manner. I continued flying for about another year and then my schedule became hectic enough that I gave it up. Another factor was the realization that I had a bad habit of letting the plane get ahead of me, and that could become a fatal mistake.

A lot of wrestlers learned to fly in the next few years. Jimmy Garvin went on to become a commercial pilot and—to my knowledge—is still flying for a feeder airline based in the Southeast. Don Curtis still flies and is both commercially licensed and jet qualified. Larry Zybysco still flies, as does Ronnie Garvin. Many of you, I am sure, remember when Buddy Colt crashed in old Tampa Bay when returning from a flight in Miami. Bobby Shane lost his life in that crash, and it effectively ended Buddy's career as a wrestling star. Gary Hart and Austin Idol survived along with Buddy. Although they were laid up for some time, they did return to the sport.

Bill Watts—"Cowboy" Bill Watts, that is—not only became a very proficient pilot, he eventually got involved with a private flying field, complete with a small terminal in Oklahoma. Sonny Myers, former wrestler, who because of age became a referee, survived a crash in his plane when he flew into almost zero visibility. He ended up flying into the ground. Myers and his passenger Tony Marino both survived, but Marino suffered a broken arm. They were flying from Tampa to Ft. Lauderdale. The idea that you did better time if you flew by private air than traveling by car appealed to wrestlers. Traveling in a car had taken too many lives and ended too many careers.

Eventually, private planes would give way to commercial plane trips. The airline industry, I am sure, offered up "if you have time to spare … then fly private air."

From the Gordon Solie Collection

Gordon had a good laugh about the reverse rib his friends pulled on him.

CHAPTER SIX
Strictly Wrestling

Grudge Match

Pain raced through his body like an express train. He grimaced and tried to fight back the waves of nausea that swept over him. He had to escape, but the problem was how? Schmidt applied more pressure, and the pain intensified to the point where he was sure he would pass out. He tried to drop to the canvas but Schmidt kept him upright. The referee asked again, "Do you give?" "No!" he said through clenched teeth. His eyes were filming over … clouding his mind. He had to break the hammerlock! In a desperation move, he raised his right arm and swung backwards with all the strength he had left. He felt the satisfying crunch as his elbow connected with the side of Schmidt's jaw.

He felt the grip on his arm go limp and sprang forward out of the hold. The crowd cheered mightily as Eddie Graham moved quickly toward the ropes in an effort to gain a valuable second of rest and years of respite. Graham turned to see Schmidt back on his feet and moving toward him.

The hatred that burned from his eyes as he moved in was intensified by the twisted expression of rage on his face. Graham watched warily as he crunched and feigned his injury a little in an attempt to throw Schmidt off guard. Schmidt was too ring-wise to fall for the trick! He stopped his advance and began to move cautiously, watching for his chance to close in on Graham and deliver the hold or a blow that would put Graham out of the match and out of wrestling, if he could.

At that instant, Graham lunged for the right leg of Schmidt. The leg dive was successful. Schmidt fell backwards onto the canvas. Graham attempted to maneuver into a step-over toe hold, but Schmidt twisted away in the bare second that he had to move. Graham tried again to pin the brawny German, but Schmidt shook him off and sprang back to his feet. Once again both men circled warily. Graham feint a leg dive and went for a headlock. Then moving with eye-escaping speed he applied a hammerlock to Schmidt. He increased the pressure, and Schmidt uttered an obscenity through pain-clenched teeth. Graham kept the pressure on. He knew he could get Schmidt to concede, but he wanted to render the arm as useless as possible. Schmidt managed, through brute strength, to stagger to the ropes and put his foot through. The referee moved in and called for the break.

Graham broke cleanly and stepped back. Schmidt whirled and dove for Graham's leg as Graham side-stepped Schmidt's move, smashing him on the back with the flat of his foot. The crowd went wild as they sensed Graham was going to close in. Graham smashed again with his foot! Schmidt tried to roll away but Graham was on him like an avenging tiger! The pain was gone, submerged by the swelling desire of victory that surged within him. Schmidt got halfway to his feet when Graham threw a full-front face lock on him, straining to break the German's facial bones and his nose. Schmidt's eyes took on a glassy look as the pain started to send his body mercifully into shock. Graham shook Schmidt like a dog would shake a dead rat! Schmidt's eyes rolled upwards as his arms dropped, and his body went limp. Graham turned the senseless body loose. Schmidt collapsed on the canvas, out cold. Graham clambered up the ring ropes in the corner onto the post. Six thousand voices lifted in a single stream of anticipation. Graham was obviously moving to his famous flying knee smash. Victory was not enough for Graham. He wanted to smash Schmidt past the point of ever wrestling again! He crouched for just a moment on the ring post ... then he sprang from the post toward the prostrate form of Hans Schmidt.

From the Gordon Solie Collection

Eddie Graham

Ted

He felt a little sleepy as he paced back and forth in the dressing room before his match with "Killer" Austin. Ted liked Florida, but it was a little too warm for him tonight. Austin was a rugged opponent who would stop at nothing to gain a victory. That didn't worry Ted too much, however. He had met tougher men in the past and would probably meet tougher men in the future. It seemed like every time a wrestling promoter had a wrestler get out of hand, he, Ted, was brought in to settle the dispute and get things back on an even keel.

He reached up and scratched his left shoulder and then sat down on the floor. He didn't bother to work out, he just waited patiently. He had worked out that afternoon and knew he was in top shape. If only he didn't feel so sleepy. He yawned broadly and thought dreamily about the hills in Canada and his friends who were enjoying a full night's sleep while he was here in Florida getting ready to wrestle. He wondered why he ever decided to get into wrestling and quickly realized that, all in all, he had it good and for the most part enjoyed the contest.

He heard Dave coming down the hall and knew that it was time for the long descent down the stairs and into the ring. He got up slowly, stifled a yawn and followed along behind Dave as they went down the stairs. The cheers started before he made it all the way down and continued until he entered the ring and the announcer said, "In this corner, weighing 242 pounds, wearing black trunks, from San Francisco, Ca., 'Killer' Austin. And in the opposite corner, also wearing black trunks, weighing 650 pounds, from Canada, 'Terrible' Ted, the Wrestling Bear." Ted just stood there and sighed softly.

From the Gordon Solie Collection

How would you like to wrestle this furry guy?

Something Left Behind

From the Gordon Solie Collection: photo by Jerry Prater

Buddy Colt (above left) and "Sputnik" Monroe battled for control.

From the Gordon Solie Collection: photo by Jerry Prater

Dory Funk Sr. was considered King of "The Texas Death Match."

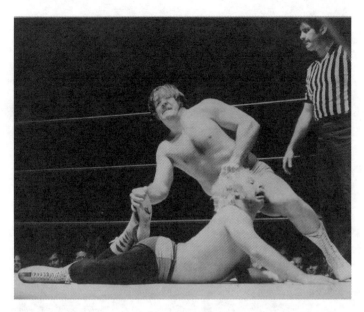

From the Gordon Solie Collection: photo by Jerry Prater

Bobby Shane's face contorted as Tim Woods pulled his leg and the hair on his head.

From the Gordon Solie Collection: photo by Jerry Prater

Dory Funk, Jr. (above right) battled many times against Jack Brisco (above left), including a classic match that ended in a one-hour draw. Gordon loved to call the action when Dory and Jack met in the squared circle.

From the Gordon Solie Collection: photo by Jerry Prater

"Big" Bill Dromo, weighing in at 260 lbs., defeated Johnny Valentine for the Southern Heavyweight Championship in 1973. Two years earlier, Bill entertained wrestling fans in Macon and Columbus, Ga., with promoter Fred Ward. Fans in Columbus saw Bill in a 15-man "Wrestle Royale" including George Scott, Derrell Cochran, Roberto Soto and Bob Armstrong.

From the Gordon Solie Collection

Bobby Duncum prevailed as the Florida Brass Knuckles Champion in 1974.

PROMOTER PAUL JONES
AND
MID-SOUTH SPORTS PRESENTS
ATLANTA
JUNE 27, 28, AND 29, 1974

LES THATCHER, PAUL JONES, GORDON SOLIE

The Right Choice for

The

WRESTLING FANS INTERNATIONAL ASSOCIATION ANNUAL CONVENTION

From the Gordon Solie Collection: WFIA program© by Norman Keitzer

From the Gordon Solie Collection

The legendary Johnny Valentine (above) applied pressure to Eddie Graham. Johnny's "heel" attitude entertained crowds where ever he performed, including when promoter Francis Fleser's World Wide Sports presented *Big Time Wrestling* events at the Cobo Arena in Detroit, Mich., (1971).

From the Gordon Solie Collection: photo by Bill Otten

Leroy Brown on his way to drop a powerful arm on Manny Fernandez

From the Gordon Solie Collection

Charlie Kalani, aka "Professor" Tanaka (above left), was about to demonstrate a martial arts chop. Outside of professional wrestling, he co-starred in more than 39 television and film roles such as the 1987 film *Running Man*, featuring fellow athletes Arnold Schwarzenegger, Jim Brown and Jesse Ventura.

From the Gordon Solie Collection: photo by Bill Otten

Mike Graham was about to belt "Bugsy" McGraw.

The Real Prophets

The prophets speak
Not from the house on the
Hill....
But from the streets.
Alas they are experts....
And the Sun Dial moves on

From the Gordon Solie Collection

Promoter "Cowboy" Luttrall moved the live wrestling matches to Tampa's Fort Homer Hesterly Armory (above) in late 1959 to accommodate larger crowds.

From the Gordon Solie Collection

From Fort Homer Hesterly Armory (Tampa) to the arena of the Bayfront Center (St. Petersburg, Fla.), the crowds attending matches for *Championship Wrestling from Florida* continued to grow.

From the Gordon Solie Collection

Gordon checked out the crowd at the Bayfront Center in St. Petersburg, Fla., before the evening's wrestling card began.

They and Me

They sense a greatness I do not own
They speak in tones sincere about destination
They see a body steeped in ego
They see a mind no longer fertile
They see not the man afraid
They see not the man who never will
The greatness is gone, the defeat is there
The only thing left is the glib tongue
Pouring out platitudes and catchy little phrases that weave him tighter and tighter in
His own web of self destruction.
He wallows in the oozy slime of self-pity and enjoys it.

From the Gordon Solie Collection: photo by Bill Otten

Nikolai Volkoff (above left) and "Bugsy" McGraw facing off in a steel chain match

The Narrow Road

Preach to me of fire and brimstone
Tell me of Hell and Damnation
Show me the narrow unpaved road to Heaven
Lead me away from cards and the lucky seven
Cure me of drink and women
Improve my posture and stop my smoke
Give me Graham on Sunday
Tithe my money and leave me broke
My only comment will be, "Well, Well, Let's all go."

From the Gordon Solie Collection

"Bugsy" McGraw became the Florida Heavyweight Champion in 1981.

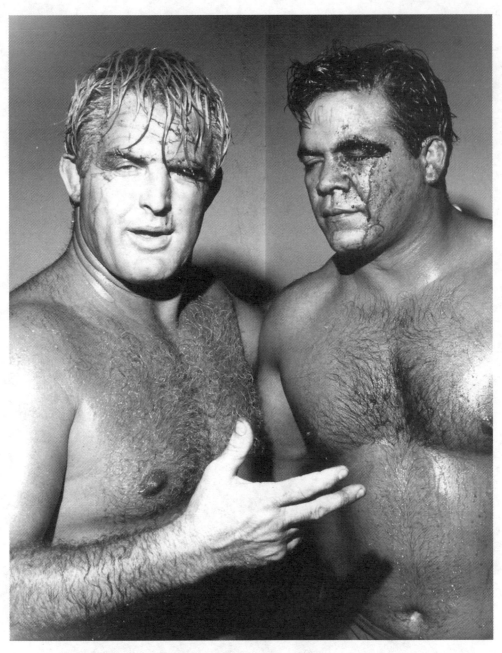

From the Gordon Solie Collection

Jose Lothario (above right) claimed numerous tag team titles, including the Florida version of the World Championship. He and teammate Eddie Graham look like they just finished a tough bout. Houston promoter Paul Boesch listed Jose on his top 10 all-time wrestlers list. Boesch said Lothario took on all comers week after week, year after year, and never disappointed the fans.

Lord Alfred Hayes squeezed a headlock on Barry Windham.

From the Gordon Solie Collection: photo by Bill Otten

From the Gordon Solie Collection: photo by Bill Otten

Gordon Solie, Bruce Thorpe and Coach John Heath applauded Eddie Graham at the microphone on a night honoring Eddie's retirement. The industry suffered a big loss upon Eddie's suicide in 1985.

The Great Thinkers

We have all become great thinkers today … we no longer look upon the world's great thinkers as any form of authority. We have become so busy mouthing the great "I"s that the real thinkers have been left to the wayside. Advertising and publicity have done much to destroy anyone's ability to think a problem, or set thereof, through clearly.

What has happened to the day when the scholar lived and learned with the teacher? What better way to learn than to live each part of a day with a great thinker?

From the Gordon Solie Collection

The Dare

One must find a point

In life where the

Trajectory must begin

The opposite arc....

To slope downward

Or refuel and change direction

If you dare!!!

From the Gordon Solie Collection: photo by Bill Otten

Jerry "The King" Lawler jumped off the ropes to pounce on his opponent.

When alligator trapping licenses became available in Florida, they were issued through a lottery system. Wrestler Steve Keirn really wanted to get a license, so he encouraged his mother and friends to apply for one to increase his odds. Steve walked into the Sportatorium office one day and was greeted by Gordon, "You owe me $385." "For what?" asked Steve. Gordon laid down his winning lottery notification.

The license included the right to have a co-hunter, which was Steve's plan all along. The co-hunters met another day at the Sportatorium and headed to Orlando, Fla., for an alligator trapping orientation. As rules were being covered, it was mentioned that guns were not allowed in the pursuit of trapping alligators. "I'm at least going to bring my .45 in case I fall out of the boat or something," piped up a concerned Gordon. This raised Steve's eyebrows. He really never planned to have Gordon in the boat with him looking for gators at night in the Everglades, and he thought that was understood.

There was only one question asked by the new licensees at the otherwise uneventful hearing. Gordon was dying for a cigarette and asked the officials, "Are we going to have a break? I really need a drink and a smoke." On the way back to Tampa, Gordon brought up the idea of his .45 again. Steve could keep still no more, "You cannot have a .45 in your pocket, a martini in one hand, a cigarette in the other hand and go alligator trapping!"

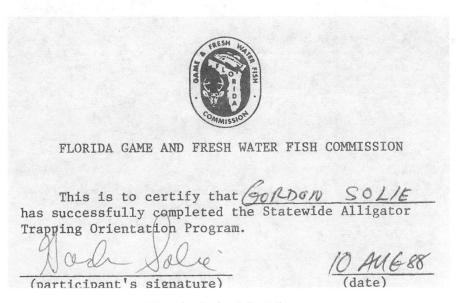

From the Gordon Solie Collection

Something Left Behind

From the Gordon Solie Collection

Steve "Gator" Keirn (above) aligned with Mike Graham to win the Florida Tag Team Championship belts in 1978. He is pictured above in the late 1980s at a Pro Wrestling Federation card.

From the Gordon Solie Collection

Brian Blair (above top) used pressure to the left arm in an effort to control Jesse Barr. In a 1982 Orlando victory over Jim Garvin, Brian took the Florida Heavyweight Championship belt.

From the Gordon Solie Collection

"Magnum TA" (above top) first became known to Florida fans as Terry Allen in the early 1980s. Terry was slated by many to become the National Wrestling Alliance World Heavyweight Champion before a car accident ended his career. Above, Terry is shown trying to lock up the face of Cyclon Negro at the Concorde Arena in Aruba. The special guest announcer was Gordon Solie.

CHAPTER SEVEN
Strictly Racing

Tortured Rubber

Tortured rubber screamed sharply against scorched asphalt and then lifted into the air. The machine arched over the slight retaining wall and rolled sideways over and over three times. The spectators screamed, a woman standing near the first turn opened her mouth to shriek and collapsed, falling forward into a farmer standing in front of her.

The red flag was being waved desperately by the starter, and all stewards in the turns, several pit men, mechanics and friends of racing rushed to the number one turn where the accident occurred. "Thank God there is no fire," one man murmured to himself as he ran to the ripped and twisted piece of metal that just seconds before had been a sleek powerful sprint car.

The car itself had come to rest finally on its side with one wheel revolving lazily. The driver had been flopped from side to side in the flipping car and now was half hanging, half sitting in the cockpit. Blood was oozing slowly from his ear and his helmet was half ripped from his head, showing more blood pouring from cuts and scrapes.

Willing hands lifted him gently from the car and stretched him out on the ground. Simultaneously, the track physician and the ambulance attendants with the stretchers arrived to rush him to the hospital. The doctor placed a stethoscope to the chest of the driver and listened intently. Somebody in the background spoke angrily, "Damn it! Put out that cigarette, you know better!"

The doctor gave instructions to the attendants; they loaded the driver on the stretcher and carried him to the ambulance. A wrecker arrived to pull the remains of the car away. The announcer calling the races continued to explain to the people still on their feet in the stands that everything that could be done for the driver would be done, and that word of his condition would be brought to them immediately as it was known. The scores of men that had rushed to the scene of the wreck now moved back to the pit area. Voices were muted by the impact of the crash and the obvious condition of the driver.

The scorers of the race were concerning themselves with placing the remaining cars into the position they were running before the accident occurred. The slips with their numbers were prepared and the announcer called them off, with the added note for the drivers to please hurry, as there was no time for delay. Pit crews rushed out and took advantage of the extra time to check tires, gas, oil, and wipe windshields of the cars. Drivers gulped a few swallows of water or Coke to quench their thirst. The starter moved up and down the homestretch straightaway, urging each man to get into his machine and get started. Push cars moved onto the track at the announcers bidding and began lining up behind the cars nearest the number one turn. One by one the drivers stepped into the cockpits, replaced their crash helmets and tightened their safety belts. The first two cars waved their push cars to shove them forward and the announcer called the order of cars again: number 3, 71, 54, 89, 66, 14, 25, 12, 77, 81, 99, 16, and 1: thirteen surging race cars where there had been fourteen! Close to one hundred thousand dollars in machinery on the track and thirteen men, who in a moment stood the chance of joining their fellow driver in the stubbled field off the track!

One by one the cars were started. Slowly they gathered into their respective positions, all of them single-file now in the exact order as called out by the starter and the announcer. As they moved out of the fourth turn onto the straightaway, the starter looked them over carefully as they began to erupt into speed. He shook his head and pointed to car number #89. The driver pulled back into line, and the starter held up one finger and waved the drivers on, signaling for one more lap. All the drivers, including the man in the cockpit of #89, held up their hands to signal one more lap. They moved like a disjointed snake into the number one turn, into number two and down the backstretch, each man holding his position and each man hoping to get the jump when the green flag was waved. Turns three and four disappeared under the wheels of the machines as each driver watched the starter intently. He returned their scrutiny, and suddenly his arm flashed and the green flag that he had hidden behind the yellow caution flag flashed into view. Each man stepped down on the accelerator, all the engines roared their answer and once again rubber screamed a tortured reply to the burning asphalt.

Thirteen cars entered the number one turn, the #3 car continued to hold the lead as #71 tried to find a groove on the outside to pass. The #1 car got the jump on #16 when the flag dropped and moved into 12th position. Kenny Randall in the Rexton Offy fought his wheel and moved #71 higher on the outside, trying to get a bite that would send him out front of the number two turn. Big Allie Buxton hunched a little forward behind the wheel of #3. He knew he had to go fast to stay in front of Randall. He knew too, that Randall would either pass him down the back stretch or would fall in behind him and start pushing him until he either moved over or lost it, like Alex had just done in the number one turn. Allie thought, "Damn that Randall, he doesn't care who gets hurt! But he did everything legal. No one could say he deliberately crossed anyone. Uh, huh, he just drove hard and fast and gave no quarter." Alex and Big Allie had been running in first and second spots with Randall running third when Alex lost it in the turn. "Lost it hell!" thought Big Allie. "Randall shoved him farther and farther into every turn until no one but a madman could hold it. Well, by God, he will either have to go around me or go over me because I am not going to be pushed," he resolved.

Randall was having a hard time finding a good groove on the outside and finally brushed the wall with his rear right tire. He corrected quickly and cursed to himself as he saw #3 pull a few feet farther out front. He poured it on as he straightened out from the number two turn and came up along side of Big Allie. No room here. That third turn was hell with a capital "H." He backed off, fell in behind Big Allie and waited. Sooner or later, if time allowed, he knew Big Allie would slip. He always did. A good boy, but he had a tendency to become hot headed and began treating the Offy he tooled like it was glued to the track. Eventually, Big Allie would spin and then Randall could grab the large money spot. Inches separated the two machines as they moved through the 3rd and 4th turns. As they headed down the home stretch, Randall was slip streaming Big Allie and trying to push him faster into the first turn. The crowd was on its feet, screaming along with the announcer as the two hurtled by with engines full out.

Randall was a mixture of emotions to the race fans. Half of them hated him with a passion and half of them loved him with equal passion, especially the female half. Randall was not a tall, dark, handsome man. He was short, blond, and with very straight regular features, average until he looked at you or smiled. His eyes were deep and green, his teeth, when he smiled, were even, and their whiteness was emphasized by his tanned face. His hair was cropped close in a crew cut, and he always managed to look neat. He was a consistent money winner and had a flair for showmanship that endeared him to some and incurred hatred in others. He had a way of saluting the crowd when he won that to many became offensive. He was always smiling, whether he finished first or last. But when he finished last, the smile drew thinly across his face instead of the rich, full curvature that existed when he won. He always acknowledged the groups in the audience but often shunned his fellow driver in front of the spectators. He never offered assistance to anyone and never went near a pile up. He refused any aid ever offered him. This combination made him a strange individual on the track. Many cheered if he lost, and an equal amount when he won. Everyone knew he was a hard driver, a merciless driver and a man who asked no quarter. He took advantage of every opportunity he could to improve his position on the track; he often had the crowd on its feet by his procedure of drifting high on the outside in the turns and brushing the walls with his tires. Randall didn't move to the outside to please the crowd, however; he moved to the outside to try to move around his competitors by using guts where brains should be.

Now he tried it again, moving to the outside, watching the wall look like a blur of white. Big Allie saw the move and continued to hold the inside slot knowing that he had to come out of the turn in front or relegate himself to second spot. He tried moving in a little faster. The rear end began to lighten, and he strained as he fought to keep the car going toward the number two turn. Randall was alongside now. Big Allie began to drift slightly to the top. Randall ignored him and continued to arch the other rim of the turn. Big Allie knew he couldn't stop Randall from going around him now. He toyed with the idea of just drifting a little farther and letting his car edge Randall into the wall. No, he couldn't do it. Not deliberately. He watched as Randall came out of the number two turn into the backstretch and pulled into the lead. Randall's grin became a little wider now as he shot for the number three turn.

The announcer was screaming hoarsely by now as he, along with the fans, watched Randall pass and go into the lead. The starter watched and thought to himself that Randall was nuts, but one hell of a driver. Randall flashed out of number four and down the home stretch, and the crowd roared! He moved smoothly now into the inside groove and wheeled through number one and two turns. Allie was right behind him; now it was his turn to wait. Allie wouldn't go to the outside to pass—you had to be nuts to go to the outside on this track. And as far as he was concerned, Randall was! Randall moved around #16 down the back stretch and Allie watched the gap between he and #71 grow wider. "What the hell," he thought. "Second place pays pretty good." For three laps, Randall continued to widen the gap, moving surely and smoothly around slower cars until he lapped three more. Allie was still second, but now he was almost a straightaway behind #71. As Randall powered out of the number four turn, again he saw the starter wave the white flag. One lap to go, he slowed down noticeably. Allie began to move up. "Damn him," thought Allie. "I suppose he's pulling the same crap again. Slowing down and making it look like he is in trouble." But Allie knew he couldn't afford to take a chance. He powered on, trying to catch the speeding Randall. You could never tell. He might be in trouble, there might be a chance. He closed the gap to a half a straightaway. Randall entered the turn and seemed to be going slower yet. Allie continued to move, faster and faster now, trying to close in and grab the first spot. Down the backstretch he caught Randall.

By now, the fans were jumping hysterically as it looked as though Allie might take the lead. But Allie knew he couldn't. Randall was playing with him, making it a show. "God, how I hate him!" thought Allie. Randall powered on just enough in the straight away to keep his two front wheels ahead of Allie as they entered the third turn. Allie had no choice; he backed off and fell behind once again. He stayed with him through the turn, and Randall powered down the homestretch to take the checkered flag. The crowd was wild! The announcer continued to shout comments into the mike but not many heard him. His voice just heightened the excitement of the fans. Randall slid through the turns and waved at the grandstand as he came down the homestretch again. He veered into his pit area and braked his machine. His crew quickly pulled the car around and backed it into the pits and began to check it over. Randall turned once again to the crowd, waved, and then sat down asking for a Coke. Allie came in and went directly to his pit. He heard the announcer call his name for second spot and heard the crowd respond but he didn't acknowledge it. The race was over. Randall won again. What the hell....

The promoter, a sharp man with a dollar, smiled briefly and nodded at the announcer to call the next group on the track for the consolation race. The feature was next and he was pleased that Randall had made such a show of the semi-final.

The resident physician at the hospital watched as the orderly stamped the papers, and then he reached down and signed them. DOA spelled the message across the papers of admission to the hospital. Alexander L. Reid, 24 years old, married, one child, age 2; died: May 22nd, 2:57 p.m. as a result of a fractured skull and broken neck incurred while racing at Smoke Hill Downs Speedway. Alex Reid would race no more. The woman who had fainted in the stands was now a widow with a child to support. Racing claimed another body for the altar of speed. For Alex Reid, the black flag would be waved....

The new widow had been placed on an emergency cot next to the emergency room and was now sleeping under sedation. Her body twitched occasionally as apparently her subconscious absorbed the information that she had feared since marrying Alex Reid three years ago. She was only 19 years old, small, five feet one in her stocking feet.

She had been brought to the hospital by one of the members of Alex's pit crew. By the time she arrived, Alex was already covered by a white sheet. No one had to tell her he was gone. She knew it instinctively the moment she saw his machine flip over the wall. Their two-year-old child, Johnny Reid, gazed around the room wide-eyed as he was held by the top mechanic for Alex, Harry Jordon. Harry answered the questions asked him by the hospital authorities while holding the child. "Yeh, he has folks, they're in Des Moines." "No, I don't know if he went to church or had a minister." "Yes, I'll notify his folks."

Meanwhile, Smoke Hill Downs Speedway was a scene of activity. Kenny Randall watched as the crew refueled the racer. He wiped his face again with a rag and waited. The big one was next. Twenty-five laps on the half-mile oval. Twenty-five times around to take home the big money for this fair. There would be another gold-plated trophy to add to the growing collection around the house. Randall thought briefly about Alex, "Wonder how he is doing." Several of the fellas in the pits had said that Alex was dead when they pulled him from the wreck. Kenny got up from the little folding stool he always had in the pits and walked over to the judge's stand. He asked Celia, one of the scorers, "Anyone know how Alex is doing?" "No word yet, Kenny," Celia replied. "I imagine we should hear something soon though." Kenny looked up soberly, "I heard some of the guys say he looked bad." "You can never tell, he might have just been knocked out and cut up," Celia answered optimistically. Kenny nodded and turned to go back to the pit, when the track physician returned in the second ambulance. Kenny strode to the door of the meat wagon and looked in at the doc. The doctor, usually a smiling, happy, little, overweight man was somber now. He shook his head at Kenny and spoke slowly, "He never knew what hit him after the first roll." "He had a fractured skull and a broken neck." Kenny's eyes narrowed briefly as he searched the doctor's face to see if he could find any recrimination there. Seeing none, he said, "Bad break," and turned to walk back to his car. Big Allie standing near by choked the word, "Killer," in his throat as Kenny passed him.

Dr. Mel Thomas hefted his frame from the ambulance and half waddled, half walked to the judge's stand. He spoke for a moment to the promoter and then turned back to the emergency vehicle. The promoter beckoned to the announcer. Gary Walch leaned away from his microphone and listened intently as the promoter spoke. "Look Gary, Alex is dead. But don't tell the people that. Just say that the exact condition is not known at this time. Got it?" Gary responded with, "Yeah, Yeah, I got it. No point in killing the crowd for the next race." The promoter came back with "Right."

Gary swung around and began to speak into the microphone. "Ladies and gentlemen, your attention please … we just now received word that the exact condition of Alex Reid is at this time still unknown. If we receive any further word, we will pass it on to you immediately. And now, may I have your attention in the pits? Get the cars on the track for the feature race please. All drivers and pit crews move them out please onto the track. This is the feature 25 lap race for the North Dakota State Championship. May we have the push cars on the track?"

Scores of men galvanized into action and began to move quickly. Drivers began putting on helmets and gloves … some wrapping their faces with white handkerchiefs to help keep the dust out of their mouths. Kenny Randall swung into the snug cock pit of the Rexton Office. He slid onto the cushioned leather seat and pulled the safety belt snugly around his waist. He reached over his shoulder and grasped the shoulder straps, pulling them into position. His pit man handed him his red helmet. Kenny put it on and let the visor of plexi-glass stay up. There it would stay until he kicked his car into the first turn. He had the pit man change the right front tire to give him a little better fit in the turns. He looked back to see if the push car was ready. He nodded an "O.K." to the driver. He grasped the brake on the left as he felt the bump of the large steel plate on the front of the push car. He pulled the brake back slightly and let the car lurch forward. The engine coughed once and then roared into the sound that meant money to Kenny Randall and thrills to the fans. He horsed the machine into the number one turn. He felt the car out carefully to see if the new tire had a beneficial effect on handling. It did feel a little snugger … good enough … this might be all the extra bite he would need. Kenny didn't think he would have to use the outside groove but you could never tell. Lots could happen out here and fast.

Randall moved out for the parade lap. The announcer was calling on the fans to take out their handkerchiefs, their hats … their programs … and wave at the drivers as they passed in front of the stand. Each driver offered his hand in salute of the spectators. This symbol was taken from ancient Rome when the Gladiators passed into the Coliseum and saluted, saying "We, who are about to die salute you." The scene of thousands of handkerchiefs, programs and hats all being waved sounded the final note to the pre-race ceremony. The 16 cars finally passed in review and the announcer thanked the crowd briefly and then once again gave a partial rundown of the first eight cars. Again, the ranks closed and the sixteen became two rows of eight.

Big Allie scowled as he saw Randall smile as usual and help his crew push the Rexton Offie out onto the surface of the track. "Damn him," he thought, "he'll sit on the pole and no one can get near him." Allie hadn't done too badly for himself, however, he was sitting pole position second row. Third fastest qualifier in the time trials! Jerry Newsome would sit on the outside first row in the feature, in car #64. Newsome was a clever driver with a hot piece of iron. Not as big an engine as either Kenny or Allie, but the car handled well and Jerry was a quick chauffeur. The announcer was calling out the positions to the audience at the time, "In the pole position by virtue of the fastest qualifying time here at the Smoke Hill Downs race meet … #71, the Rexton Offie driven by Kenny Randall … on the outside in car #64, Jerry Newsome in the Modified Chevy … second row pole position … Big Allie Buxton in car #3. Big Allie was a second place finisher in over all point standings last year. On the outside second row, in car number 38 … another powerful Offenhauser … Crash Barker…." The announcer continued to give the line up to the fans as the pit crews and drivers continued to move their swift racers onto the track. The starter was going down the line checking to make sure that all safety equipment was in order. Not too much need really, these men were all professionals and realized the value of safety equipment.

The push cars began to start some of the leaders. The sudden popping and roar of the engines added the extra touch of excitement the crowds anticipated. One by one, the powerful cars began to move around the track as each driver re-adjusted himself to the car and the track conditions. Now all of them were moving around the oval and the starter signaled for the men to get into their positions. Each man found his spot and soon sixteen machines controlled by sixteen men were lined up two by two. Eight rows of compressed speed, waiting now for the parade lap … then the final pace lap and the green flag. At the end of the 12 miles of racing, lay money … adulations … and a cold beer.

Kenny checked his instruments as he went into the number three turn and revved his engine to clear the carburetors. Everything looked okay. He glanced to his side and smiled at Jerry Newsome in #64. Jerry nodded and looked away toward the starter. Kenny paced the pack out of the number four and tensed for the green flag. He accelerated slowly at first and then as he felt the starter would drop the flag, he shoved his foot down hard. The machine snapped forward just as the green flag dropped. Once again, Kenny had timed his maneuver correctly. That split-second advantage was enough to give him an extra ten feet of running room. Jerry nosed in quickly and fell in behind him, liking the inside groove better. Sixteen racers began to bunch as they hit the first turn. Randall was all by himself in the turn, but behind him men fought to maintain positions and shook off the jarring of wheels hitting wheels. Horsing the wheel, Kenny moved into number two and down the back stretch. Jerry hung on grimly in the turn and faded slightly as they came down the back chute. Randall could outrun him in the straightaway. Just then Big Allie passed Jerry on the right. Allie always looked grim whether he was on or off the track. Kenny decided that Allie wasn't a very happy guy. For some reason, Kenny started to think about Alex. Poor guy, he got the black flag.

For that brief moment as he let his mind wander, a mistake was about to happen as the car came upon the same turn where Alex Reid crashed. Was it a mistake or retribution? Now, a second black flag would wave at Smoke Hills Downs Speedway.

From the Gordon Solie Collection

In 1950, Tampa's Speedway Park hosted "The Cigar Bowl Race." The feature race was won by Frank Luptow (center front). Gordon, on assignment for WEBK Radio, can be seen in the back row holding the microphone.

From the Gordon Solie Collection

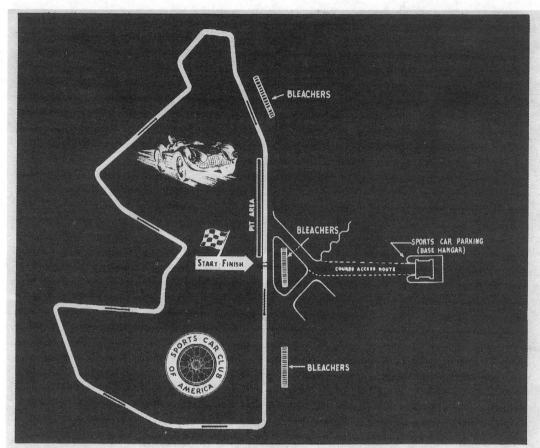

ROUTING...

Florida National Sports Car Races are being held at MacDill Air Force Base in Tampa. The base is located at the southernmost end of the peninsula jutting into Tampa Bay, and may be reached by driving south on West Shore Blvd. or Route 600.

From the North: From Jacksonville follow U.S. 90 west to Lake City. Take U.S. 41 south from Lake City down to Tampa.

From the Northwest: From Tallahassee take U.S. 319 south to U.S. 98. Go east on U.S. 98 to Perry. Take U.S. Alt. 27 (U.S. 19/98) southeast to Chiefland. From Chiefland, continue south on U.S. 98 to Brooksville, then U.S. 41 into Tampa.

From the East: Pick up U.S. 92 at Kissimmee (17 mi. south of Orlando), and go west to Tampa.

From the South: Take U.S. 41 north to Tampa.

ADMISSION AND PARKING

$1.00 Advance, $1.50 at the gate on Race Day. Children under 12 accompanied by parents or other responsible people, will be admitted free.

A large free parking area will be available on the field for all cars.

From the Gordon Solie Collection

One of Gordon's fond memories was announcing stock car races at MacDill Air Force Base.

SCHEDULE of EVENTS

9:45 A.M.
Imperial Polk County Race
50 Miles—Modified Cars of less than 1500 C.C.

11:00 A.M. and 12:00 NOON
Protestant Services at Chapel Nos. 1 and 3

11:00 A.M. and 12:00 NOON
Catholic Mass at Chapel No. 2
Free bus transportation will be available to the Church of your choice on the Base.

12:30 P.M.
Festival of States Race
50 Miles—Modified Cars of more than 1500 C.C.

1:45 P.M.
Gasparilla Trophy Race
50 Miles—Production Cars

2:40 P.M.
Billy Mitchell Drill Team presents the Queen
General Mooney Crowns the Queen

3:00 P.M.
Governor Dan McCarty Memorial Race
200 Miles—All Classes and Categories

★ ★ ★

RACING FLAGS AND WHAT THEY MEAN

GREEN FLAG — The race has started, the course is clear.

YELLOW—Motionless—Take care, danger, NO PASSING.

YELLOW—Waved—Great danger, be prepared to stop, NO PASSING.

RED FLAG—Stop immediately, clear the course.

BLUE—Motionless—Another competitor is following you closely.

BLUE—Waved—Another competitor is trying to pass you. MAKE ROOM.

YELLOW—With Vertical Red Stripes—Take Care. Oil has spilled on the road.

WHITE—An ambulance or service car is on the circuit.

BLACK—Stop at your pit.

CHECKERED—You have finished the race.

From the Gordon Solie Collection

For a time, Gordon managed the radio station for the University of Tampa to help pay for class tuition toward a degree in microbiology. He stopped in at closing one evening and asked his assistant, Jim Gallagher, to go with him to the Hank Snow concert at Tampa's McKay Auditorium. As the two were backstage, they heard the crowd going wild over the opening act … a young man by the name of Elvis Presley. Jim still credits Gordon for passing on some broadcasting tips, especially when it comes to auto racing. For years fans have been known to bring FM radios to the track so they can simultaneously watch the race and listen to Jim Gallagher, "the Voice of Sebring."

From the Gordon Solie Collection

From the Gordon Solie Collection

In 1958, Al Sweeney asked Gordon to announce the IMCA races at the Florida State Fairgrounds. Drivers came from across the United States to compete in the IMCA Midwinter Championship. Sweeney was later inducted into the National Sprint Car Hall of Fame. His name appeared below Gordon's on the 1959 program (above).

HILLSBORO COFFEE COMPANY
3412 E. Broadway   Phone 4-3366   Tampa, Florida

COFFEE   TEA   SPICES
We Cater to Hotels, Restaurants, Concessions

EVENT NO. 1

QUALIFYING TIME TRIALS—Conditions: Distance, One Lap. Drivers limited to three test laps of course. Time established in this event determines starting positions in events to follow.

Car No.	Driver	Name of Car	City	Time
2	Pete Folse	Offenhauser	Tampa, Fla.	
C-2	Don Carr	Offenhauser	St. Petersburg, Fla.	
K-2	Jack Rounds	Offenhauser	Huntington Park, Cal.	
"2-A	Johnny Roberts	Wayne	Wheeler, Mich.	
3	Jerry Blundy	Offenhauser	Galesburg, Ill.	
W-3	Johnny Pouelson	Offenhauser	Gardena, Cal.	
4	Leon Clum	Offenhauser	Wapakoneta, Ohio	
4-W	Ken Wines	Wayne	Indianapolis, Ind.	
8	Bob Marshman	Dodge	Yerkes, Pa.	
14	Mickey McCormick	Offenhauser	Hutchinson, Kansas	
17	Colby Scroggins	DeSoto	Pasadena, Cal.	
19	Wild Bill Waters	Offenhauser	Rushville, Ind.	
22	James Carroll	Wayne	Syracuse, N. Y.	
24	Will Cagle	Corvette	Tampa, Fla.	
26	James Murphy	Offenhauser	South Haven, Mich.	
29	Red Amick	Chevrolet	Muncie, Ind.	
L29	Bob Luscomb	Offenhauser	Orlando, Fla.	
34	Sam Annunziatta	Hal	Tampa, Fla.	
45	Eddie Bond	Mercury	Bedford, Ind.	
47	Arbie Hensley	Studebaker	Richmond, Ky.	
49	Hugh Randall	Cadillac	Louisville, Ky.	
55	Bud Randall	Offenhauser	Mitchell, Ind.	
61	Leon Hubble	Offenhauser	Indianapolis, Ind.	
66	Bob Tattersall	Wayne	Streator, Ill.	
67	Jim Hurtibise	Offenhauser	Gardena, Cal.	
69	Harvey Konkel	GMC	Milwaukee, Wis.	
70	Cotton Farmer	Offenhauser	Fort Worth, Texas	
71	Buzz Barton	Offenhauser	Tampa, Fla.	
77	Wally Roberts	Wayne	Des Moines, Iowa	
91		Wayne	Harrodsburg, Ky.	
98	LeRoy Neumeyer	Offenhauser	Compton, Cal.	
99	Eddie Loetscher	Offenhauser	St. Louis, Mo.	

From the Gordon Solie Collection

The first two of four IMCA sanctioned events held in Tampa at the Florida State Fairgrounds were won by Pete Folse to kick off the 1959 season. Folse, an extremely popular Tampa driver, went on to win the '59 IMCA championship by tallying 3,885 points, more than runner up Jim Hurtubise with 2,293 points.

For the third consecutive year, Gordon announced the IMCA races at the Florida State Fairgrounds in Tampa. The ribbon cutting ceremony on opening day is shown below.

From the Gordon Solie Collection

National Speedways Inc. personnel above, from left to right: Homer Claytor, Gene Van Winkle, Johnny Hicks, Manuel Llauget, Lucille Van Winkle, "Husky" Huskisson (Secretary-manager of the Florida State Fair), Brunch Sweeney, Polly Roat, Andy Hahn, Gordon and Al Sweeney.

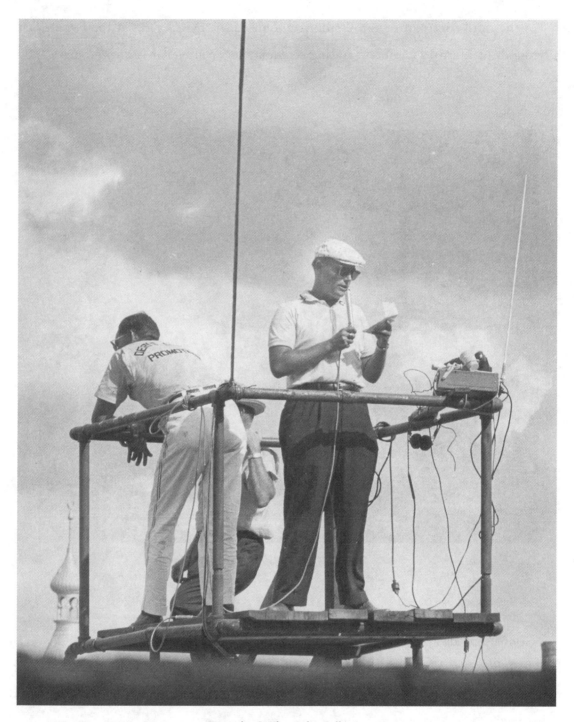

From the Gordon Solie Collection

Gordon handled the public relations and announcing duties at Phillips Field's (the old Florida State Fairgrounds) stock car races for Dery Sports Promotions in 1961. A spire from the University of Tampa is visible in the background.

After the 1961 regular season ended at Phillips Field, Gordon developed a "special day" for more stock car action, and promoter Frank Dery backed the idea. Tampa Mayor Julian Lane (seated) is pictured below receiving a proclamation to sign for "Pete Folse Day." Standing from left to right were racing publicity director, Gordon, Greater Tampa Chamber of Commerce sports committee director, Bob Carlton, and the man who presented the proclamation to Pete Folse, Jack Champlin.

From the Gordon Solie Collection: photo by A.C. McCarthy

Pete Folse was recognized for his outstanding IMCA racing performance, and the positive feedback he created for the city of Tampa. Al Sweeney, president of National Speedways, Inc., was present to honor Pete for his third consecutive IMCA title.

Frank Dery and Gordon combined the Folse award ceremony with a triple feature of racing at the Florida State Fairgrounds. Unfortunately for Pete, he blew an engine in the first heat and was done driving for the day. Buzz Barton, who finished second to Folse in the IMCA standings, was expected to be stiff competition in the super-modified feature race. The 3,000 fans honoring Folse that day watched Roy Robbins of Louisville, Ken., take the modifieds and Dick Hope of Tampa capture the late model division.

Gordon, however, was not done announcing or promoting for the '61 season. In November, Gordon and Frank Dery put on the first "100 Lap Florida Century Championships" at the Florida State Fairgrounds. It was a 1-2-3 finish for Dick Hope, Will Cagle and Buzzie Reutimann respectively.

A collision in 1961 on the track at Phillips Field is shown below.

From the Gordon Solie Collection: Tampa Tribune staff photo by Art Thomas

From the Gordon Solie Collection: Tampa Tribune staff photo by Art Thomas

Cush Revette, above left in the 1955 Chevy, almost flipped as his drive shaft split, the right rear wheel came off, and he spun in front of Al Ackerman in the white 1961 Dodge Lancer. G.E. King chauffeured the dark car (far right) in the 100 Lap "Century Race."

From the Gordon Solie Collection: Tampa Tribune staff photo by Dan Fager

Gordon was pointing out last-minute instructions to contractor Sam Bliven in 1962 as the construction of Golden Gate Speedway and Sports Mecca neared completion. Frank Dery relied on Gordon, three insurance companies and his own business knowledge to bring a new race track to the city of Tampa. In addition to being part owner, Gordon was general manager and track announcer.

Tom McEwen, retired sports editor for *The Tampa Tribune*, said he believed Gordon was even better at stock car race announcing than he was at calling the action for wrestling matches.

Gordon sent this press release from Golden Gate Speedway: 1962

"A NEAR CAPACITY CROWD WATCHED WARM UP AND PRACTICE LAPS THIS AFTERNOON AT GOLDEN GATE SPEEDWAY IN TAMPA AS DRIVERS PREPPED FOR THE NASCAR GRAND NATIONAL TOMORROW.

TIME TRIALS TOMORROW WILL START AT NOON WITH 10-LAP HEATS SCHEDULED FOR 2 P.M.   THE 200-LAP FEATURE EVENT OVER THE ONE-THIRD MILE TRACK WILL GET UNDER WAY FOLLOWING THE HEAT LAPS.

AMONG THE FAVORITES ARE NASCAR CHAMPION JOE WEATHERLY …GLEN (FIREBALL) ROBERTS … REX WHITE … AND DICK PETTY.

THE GRAND NATIONAL WILL BE THE FIRST NASCAR SPONSORED RACE RUN IN TAMPA."

From the Gordon Solie Collection

"Motorsports Images & Archives Photography. Used with permission."

Above is the pre-race lineup for the November 11, 1962, NASCAR Grand National race at Golden Gate Speedway; on the right is the pole position winner, Rex White in the (#4) '62 Chevrolet and Jim Paschal on the outside (left, #41) in the Petty Engineering '62 Plymouth. It was a good day for the Petty team; Jim Paschal finished second behind Richard Petty, and Maurice Petty took sixth place. Joe Weatherly, the reigning NASCAR champion at the time, came in third.

The next day, *The Tampa Tribune* reported the spectacular teamwork demonstrated by Richard Petty and Jim Pascal. Early in the race, the two 1962 Pontiacs converged on the lead car, a red '62 Pontiac chauffeured by Buck Baker. Paschal cut inside of Baker and Petty cut inside of Paschal. "The three cars locked together and wobbled down the front straightway. Just before they went into the south turn, Paschal appeared heading into the infield out of control, but Petty pulled up, slammed into the front end of Paschal's car and straightened it out."

In addition to watching NASCAR regulars including Rex White, Ned Jarrett and "Fireball" Roberts, Tampa stock car fans enjoyed seeing local drivers Possum Jones and Buzzie Reutimann finish seventh and eighth respectively.

Something Left Behind

From the Gordon Solie Collection

Always promoting, Gordon is pictured above showing off the 6'2" trophy that he and Frank Dery planned to give away at Golden Gate Speedway to the 1962 season point leader in the late model division.

From the Gordon Solie Collection: Trademark usage courtesy of the Coca-Cola Company

As president of Suncoast Speedways, Inc., Gordon handled the promotion of stock car races for three tracks. He and Frank Dery contracted to bring NASCAR Midgets to Sunshine Speedway and Golden Gate in 1963. Gordon introduced figure-8 racing to Sunshine Speedway (St. Petersburg, Fla.) in 1964. The closest figure-8 track at the time was in Nashville, Tenn. Action from figure-8s is shown below.

From the Gordon Solie Collection: Photo published by The Coca Cola Company

Courtesy of the Tampa Tribune: photo by Bill Wilson

The 34-year-old racing promoter (Gordon, above) was checking out photos for stock car racing. Along with NASCAR events, figure-8s and 200-lap Florida late model stock car championships, Gordon and Frank Dery provided a variety of entertainment to the Suncoast such as; USAC (United States Auto Club) midgets with "Indy" drivers, Chuck Rodee, Bobby Grim, Don Branson and Allen Crowe; powder puff derbies; Dan Fleenor and the "Hurricane Hell Drivers;" action at Sunshine Dragstrip featuring Marvin Schwartz and Art Malone; and the annual stunt driving and auto crash contest at Golden Gate Speedway, aired on ABC-TV's *Wide World of Sports*.

Emil Reutimann (below) took the checkered flag victory lap at Golden Gate Speedway. An accident later claimed Emil's life on the way to the track, but he had already started a Reutimann racing legacy; son Buzzie was one of the youngest drivers to compete in the NASCAR Grand National race at Golden Gate Speedway; son Wayne can be found in the Florida State Late Model Championships history; and grandson David Reutimann debuted in the NASCAR Craftsman Truck Series in 2004 after running the Busch Series the previous year.

Photo courtesy of Gordon Solie Enterprises, Inc.

Wayne Reutimann's victory in the 200-lap Florida State Late Model Championship at Golden Gate Speedway in 1965 included the revered "Governor's Cup." He fought off Alabama's Bobby Allison for the last 150 laps. Allison couldn't be at the qualifying heats and worked his way up from a 17th starting position to within a bumper of winning.

The "Governor's Cup" was inscribed with the name "Al Keller." Al chauffeured cars owned by Frank Dery at Speedway Park and other Florida tracks before qualifying for the 1961 Indy 500. He finished fifth behind the winner, A.J. Foyt, Jr. A tragic accident during a 1961 hundred lapper in Arizona claimed Al Keller's life.

Photo courtesy of Gordon Solie Enterprises, Inc.

Jim Gray (#2) passed on the inside with Ray Bontrager (#0jr) coming on strong behind him at Golden Gate Speedway. Gray captured 10th place in the 1971 "Governor's Cup" race, while Bontrager finished in the eighth spot in both 1974 and 1976.

Photo courtesy of Gordon Solie Enterprises, Inc.

Pancho Alvarez, above right, gave the winning driver a feature race trophy. After competing for years as a successful driver, Pancho took over as racing director at Golden Gate Speedway.

Photo courtesy of Gordon Solie Enterprises, Inc.

Will Cagle (#97 above) was trying to gain on Dick Pratt at Golden Gate Speedway. The two chauffeurs competed for top prizes often on Tampa tracks. In the inaugural season at the "Gate," Cagle took the championship in the super modified division. Pratt won championships in Ohio and Indiana before heading to Florida's Suncoast.

Photo courtesy of Gordon Solie Enterprises, Inc.

Bill McCormack celebrated a victory at Golden Gate Speedway

Something Left Behind

Photo courtesy of Gordon Solie Enterprises, Inc.

Dave Breakfield (above) started competing at Golden Gate while he was still a Tampa high school student in the late 1960s. He received the "Rookie of the Year" award in the Tornado division and then moved up to a '65 Chevelle for the next season. Jim Grace (pictured below) drove the Breakfield car until Dave turned 18 and was eligible to compete.

Photo courtesy of Gordon Solie Enterprises, Inc.

From the Gordon Solie Collection

The technical advisor for the feature-length movie *Jump* was Gordon Solie (above second from left). Gordon arranged to have racing scenes filmed at Pasco County Speedway and Golden Gate Speedway in 1970. Cannon Production used the picture below of stock car action at Golden Gate Speedway to promote the movie. Actor Tom Legion portrayed "Chester Jump," the driver of the #21 stock car.

From the Gordon Solie Collection

In early 1972, *The Daredevil*, a Ken Murray production, was filmed entirely on location in the Tampa Bay area complete with a gala premier at Tampa Theatre. It was the second time Gordon served as technical advisor for a motion picture.

The Finale

The road running is over

The crowds have dissipated to their own environment

The circular track lay gathering grass and weeds

The stars have scattered to familiar clines

The promoters measure in black and red

While spectators forget what was seen and done

Lives have been changed

Visions affected

Each has a new dream

Each buries an old

The season is over

Time's come to an end

Time now to measure in black and red

CHAPTER EIGHT
Head Shots

The Fascia Sea

Have you ever noticed how faces change over the years?
How eventually the inner spirit emerges in the lines and the
Contours of the human countenance?
We cannot seem to grasp this in ourselves but it becomes painfully
Obvious when we scan those photos of yesterday.
There is so much more beauty in the face that has experienced life,
Not just tasted or toyed but truly experienced.
Faces that have seen the six year old spread-eagled on the pavement,
Blood welling from 6 places in the head.
Faces that have watched in wonder the ageless eyes of a 14 month old gazing at the sea.
Faces that have seen the contorted expressions of physical rapture
Of a mate enjoying the act of sex.
Faces that have seen the grimace of the alcoholic.
Faces that have understood the tired gentle patience of the old.
Faces that have seen the neurotic faces of the hurriers.
Strip away the facade … let the spirit emerge … remove the bondages of society….
There is nothing so wrong in being a human.
Let us stop trying to mimic the machines … the creators are becoming the created.
The largest and hardest encounter is that of acceptance.
Look back in literature….
We are what we are, what we are….

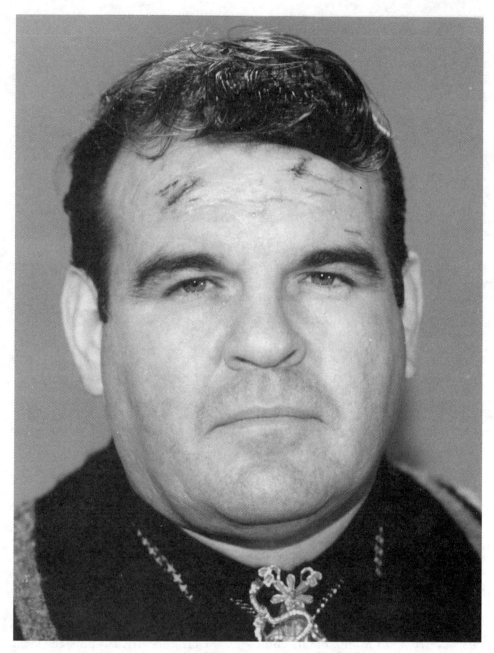

From the Gordon Solie Collection

Jack Brisco was asked to describe the toughest wrestler he ever faced. He said, "Well, the meanest was the 'Missouri Mauler'." (pictured above) "In a match one night, the 'Mauler' (Larry Hamilton) simultaneously punched me in the eye and kicked me in the stomach," stated Jack. "My eye was swelling, I had the dry heaves, and he was coming at me again. The 'Stomper' left a few holes in my chest, too."

From the Gordon Solie Collection

Archie "The Stomper" Gouldie, a student of Canadian wrestling legend Stu Hart, combined his talent with Cyclon Negro to take the NWA World Tag Team title in a 1966 San Francisco bout.

From the Gordon Solie Collection

Paul Jones won the Florida Heavyweight Championship in May of 1972 as an unmasked wrestler. He literally made waves when he threw one of his Florida Heavyweight victory belts from the Gandy Bridge into the waters of Tampa Bay. Around 1980, Paul donned the mask and wrestled as "Mr. Florida."

Head Lines

The lines appear
Cracking the visage
Each one telling a different message
Happy lines by curved lips
Tell of smiles and laughter often heard
Perpendicular lines so near the brow
Worries then … forgotten now
Across the forehead wavy lines
Speak of concentration and decline
Each line remains to tell a tale
Increase the interest each man to know
A life is told by lines
Be they yours or be they mine.

From the Gordon Solie Collection

"Thunderbolt" Patterson took the Florida Heavyweight belt in 1976. Texas fans packed houses in the early '70s to watch "King Thunderbolt" face off in main events against opponents such as "Iron Claw" Fritz Von Erich and "Ted the Wrestling Bear."

From the Gordon Solie Collection: photo by Jerry Prater

Harley Race won the NWA World Heavyweight Title eight times. Floridians witnessed world title clashes between Harley and Dusty Rhodes at spectacular events like "Hollywood Star Wars" (at the Hollywood, Fla., Sportatorium) and "The Last Tangle in Tampa" (at Tampa Stadium).

From the Gordon Solie Collection

"Cowboy" Bill Watts triumphed as the Florida Heavyweight Champion in 1974. The year before, Bill entertained fans at Atlanta's Omni where he combated "Mr. Wrestling" (Tim Woods) for the Georgia Heavyweight Championship.

From the Gordon Solie Collection

President Jimmy Carter had fun trying out a headlock on "Mr. Wrestling II" (Johnny Walker). The above photo was used to promote *Global Wrestling* where Gordon co-hosted shows with Ann Gunkel.

From the Gordon Solie Collection

Ray Candy was also known to fans as "Kareem Muhammad" when he partnered with Alijah Akeem Ambulakila (also known as Leroy Brown) to form the "Zambuie Express" tag team.

Existence

There is a particular beauty in the process of aging
To look upon one who is gradually losing the fight for survival
And see the chemical progress of death creeping over them.
At the same time you see the visage that is lined with all
Of the complicated businesses of living.
The joy lines
The worry lines
Lines of dissipation
Lines of toil and nature.
Lines caused by preliminary fights that ultimately
Lead to the final fight that we can never win.
You can look upon an old person and feel a potpourri
Of emotions for them.
Hate … fear … pity … respect … gladness … a deep, deep sympathy.
And love …. a love that knows not itself.
Just a love of a fellow being that has struggled so much longer
Than you … and knows the battle is all but over … and yet
Hangs tenaciously to the precipice over the long dark valley.
Every day life becomes just a little more dear … a little
Less adjusted to the idea of death.
You suddenly discover there are so many things to do….
So many things to say and see….
And you have so much time to reflect upon.
The universal waste of life and living … such a waste…
Such a pity and yet so human.

From the Gordon Solie Collection

Jack Brisco's eyes watered when he saw this picture of Frank Hester. Frank was one of wrestling's many travel tragedies. After wrestling on the same card with Jack one evening, Frank was killed in an auto accident near Dickson, Tenn. For the wrestlers traveling together on the circuit, each death was like losing a family member.

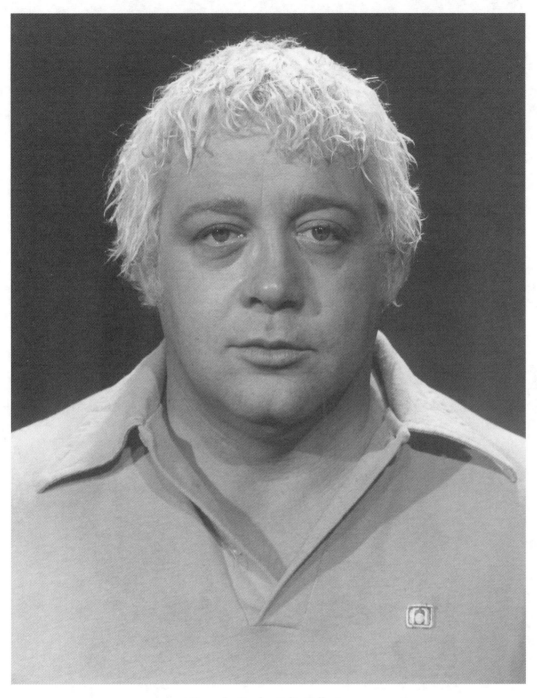

From the Gordon Solie Collection

The first Florida Television Champion was Ray "The Crippler" Stevens (above) in 1956. Ray went on to NWA World Tag Team titles with different partners including Greg "The Hammer" Valentine, Jimmy Snuka and Ivan Koloff.

From the Gordon Solie Collection

Here are a few head shots above from a "Sir Oliver Humperdink" stable. From left to right are Roger Smith (Assassin #2), Randy (R.T.) Tyler, Sir Oliver, Jody Hamilton (Assassin#1), Tetsuo Sekigawa (aka Mr. Pogo, and above as the Ninja), and Sergeant Jacques (Rene) Goulet.

From the Gordon Solie Collection: from the files of Ross Parsons © by Rogo Corporation

The team of manager Sol Weingeroff (above left), "Sputnik" Monroe (above center) and Karl Von Brauner (above right) was called an "unholy alliance" in the 1967 edition of the *Championship Wrestling Annual*. Karl and "Sputnik" had the distinction of "the most hated tag team" after only one match together.

Pure Mediocrity

Why do we seek the truth?
We wonder why we have child killers.
We scream our fears in books, lectures,
On radio and T.V.
The read minds are usurped by green
The mediocre reign supreme
Fallout has us that's for sure
My, I'm glad I'm so pure!

From the Gordon Solie Collection: photo from "The Grapevine" © by Jerry Prater/Grapevine Publishing

Roses

I can never offer you the wisdom of Socrates or Thoreau. These men and others of their makeup possess wisdom and a greatness that only comes with true humility and non-materialism. I have awakened too late to find the tremendous peace of a soul unfettered by convention; Materialism, Egoism and Machinism. I fight for reason with those who are supposed to be dearest to me. I am selfish. There is perhaps a truth here ... I offer you my rationalization that I cannot be true to anyone or anything until I am true to myself. This problem of finding one's self is no small or minor situation.

I cannot believe that it is a matter of ego. Perhaps in my own case this is true, but it is something stirring within that refuses to be stopped. I have fought for something THAT is still unanswered. I have found an inspiration. Now perhaps with the written word, I will find the kind of success I need. Perhaps this will offer the outlet. The ability for expression of one's own feelings is so often lost by the machines we now worship. I must prove my existence. There must be blades of grass. There must also be dandelions and roses. Where, if anywhere, I fit, is the problem I must solve.

Am I a blade of grass? Grass is a very necessary and a wonderful existence. Am I too a dandelion? They are good for wine. A rose I do not think you will find me; much too pure and much too beautiful. To be a rose you must be special indeed. Christ, Van Gogh, Gandhi, Socrates, these are the roses. Rare and beautiful, yet fragile in life while possessing the strongest kind of everlasting beauty. One never forgets the trueness of the rose. It will remain for a lifetime in the mind.

As if we could only all be roses.

Parking Lot Egos

Larry Corvan and his wife, Thelma, left the club just 15 minutes before last call for alcohol and walked to their Mercedes 300D in the parking lot. Al Tedelset and Vic Zabo stood on the darkened side of the row of cars, dimly lit by the ghostly mercury vapor sentinel lights. As Corvan and his wife approached, Larry staggered just a little, and Thelma chided him and mentioned stopping for coffee and eggs on the way home. Larry was not drunk, but he did have the heady feeling close to one too many. Thelma, dressed in a neat-fitting pants suit of the Silver's name, went to her side of the car as Larry dug for his keys. Their marriage, coupled with women's lib, alleviated the need for him to open her door. Unknown to them, the two men in the dark were watching their every move.

They walked from the dark side and were talking about the Dodgers game that day as they approached the 300D from the rear. They split to either side of the car. Thelma and Larry both had a quick sense of apprehension which turned to fear as Zabo, with practiced hands swiftly cupped his hand over her mouth, while he pinned her arms to her sides with his free arm. Tedelset quickly flashed an eight-inch switch blade into the coat of Larry and as calmly as the adrenaline in his body would allow him to speak, said, "Turn around, put your hands on the top of the car." Al stepped back a half step to allow Larry room to turn. As Larry partially turned, he heard Vic say to his wife, Thelma, "Baby, you and me are going to take a nice little ride…."

Larry's right fist was balled and as he continued his turn, his right arm arced and caught Al in the genitals. The knife slipped from Al's fingers as his body doubled forward trying to stop the nausea that exploded from his groin, now covering his lower abdomen. As Al's head began to reach his waist, Larry pulled Al's head downward with his hands and drove his knee into Al's face. The knee cap hit the front teeth in Al's mouth and forced its way to the incisors. As Al's head turned sideways, the jaw twisted and broke, and Al suddenly knew no more pain as he pitched to the Copper Koto asphalt surface. The partially digested meal of that night, started to spew from his mouth, mingled with parts of his broken teeth mixed with blood from his smashed lips and mouth. His head bounced off the side of the Mercedes' rear door and came to rest along with his 6-foot frame next to the left rear wheel. Bits of bile, partially digested peas, carrots and beef along with the blood and broken teeth became his pillow.

Vic watched in disbelief as Al was destroyed and tried to choose a course of action. To release Thelma was obviously the first thought and then to run! But could he get away? To get to the knife meant he would have to release her arms. He gambled. He won. Thelma was in a state of near shock. He suddenly released her arms, keeping his right hand over her mouth and in seemingly one motion, pulled his knife, hitting the spring load at the same time. He brought his left hand with the knife to her throat.

As Larry turned toward Vic and Thelma, his face still expressing his unbelief at what he had done, he heard Vic repeating in an almost chant. "Come near me and I'll kill her. Come near me and I'll kill her." He could see the point of the knife barely touching the skin on Thelma's neck.

An impasse was made. To attack was too much of a gamble. To wait for the club to close and panic the man was also too much of a gamble. Illogical reason was his only hope! Larry spoke calmly, "Look, my friend, my wife's life is more important to me than what money I have or her rings. I will put my valuables along with her purse and rings on the hood of the car. I will then turn my back, while you release her. Take the wallet and rings and go!" Vic was not without loyalty. He asked, "What about my buddy?" Larry's comeback was, "Take him with you—or leave him. I promise I will put my wife in the car and leave him there. I will not call the police and when I am gone you can gather him up and leave if you wish." Larry sensing that he now held the upper hand pushed a little harder. "If you don't make up your mind, people will be coming to the lot in a moment and then you will have new problems!"

Vic understood that reasoning! "O.K. O.K. put your wallet on the hood." He grabbed the small dinner bag that Thelma was carrying. "Put your rings in the bag," he commanded! Thelma in an almost stupor, complied. "Turn around," Vic's voice almost crackled. Now, he was in command! Larry turned slowly. Vic released Thelma, grabbed the bag, the wallet and skirted between the next two rows of cars in the darkness.

Larry quickly embraced Thelma, feeling a strange surge of sensuality as he felt her body begin to rock with strange rhythms. "Oh baby, in the car, come," he said softly as he guided her into the front seat. Quickly he got to the other side and got in behind the wheel. He didn't wait for the gas to prime before he turned the key and started the engine. The familiar sound of marbles falling in a dishpan brought back some semblance of normal everyday life.

The temptation was there to roll his car backward and forward over the head of the helpless Al on the asphalt. Instead he pulled out, his eyes straining to see if the other assailant was gone. All four doors were locked. Thelma was still in shock as he drove directly to the exit.

He still couldn't believe what he had done in the moments behind him. His disbelief was coupled with his knowledge that he was not a violent man. His children thought him so. Thelma thought him to be that way. But he knew he wasn't! Reason began to overtake his mind, the alcohol that gave him the courage was now gone. He reached into his left hand pocket for a cigarette. "Damn, I put them on the hood!" The center console offered a partially crumpled pack. He sought out a slightly bent St. Moritz and pushed in the lighter. Igniting the no-filtered end, he offered it to Thelma. Her voice was almost matter of fact, "Thank you honey." He grunted and pulled another bent smoke from his pack. Relighting the lighter, he then took a long drag.

Thelma questioned him. "Where are we going?" Assertively, Larry answered her, "To the police station of course!" "But you said you wouldn't." Larry retorted her with a, "So?" Sounding grateful, Thelma reminded him, "Well they did let us go!" "Ha," said Larry, "through no choice of his!" She begged him, "Please, let's go home." Sharply Larry asked, "Are you joking? He has your purse, $300 of my money, my credit cards, my 1800 Omega and my rings! NO WAY!" The rest of the trip was in complete silence save for a sporadic outburst of, "We are lucky! We are lucky!" Larry shrugged in non-agreement.

"Name?" "Lawrence T. Corvan." "Age?" "Forty-five" "Address?" "1718 Park Drive." "Occupation?" "Manufacture's Rep." After that standard repertoire, Larry asked in an agitated voice, "Look, I realize you have questions to ask, but what about the two men? You may still be able to pick up one of them." That possibility was already real: Al Tedelset was dead.

—

Tedelset's body was being removed by an ambulance summoned by the police, who in turn had responded to a call from Barry Sloane, an attorney at law. Sloane's Sedan Deville had crushed Tedelset's still breathing inert form when the car started to pull out of the lot. Sloane was brought to headquarters just as Corvan and his wife were leaving. "We'll be in touch after we check it out," Sgt. Rilmore said with a smile as he escorted Larry and Thelma past the booking desk. At the desk, Patrolman Wm. Registo nodded routinely to Officer Gotch. "What do you have Harry?" "Depends on the breathalyzer test whether accident or manslaughter." "Get his valuables and then give him the test." "Did you read him his rights?" "Yeah, yeah, he's an attorney, no problem."

Sloane emptied his pockets and stood there beginning to sweat. He knew he would fail the test. "O.K., Mr. Sloane, step this way." "Wait a minute, what about my wife?" "We haven't charged her, do you want us to?" "Don't be a smart bastard," he belted back. Losing his balance, he fell face forward, his forehead smacking sharply off the polished terrazzo floor. "He tripped." "No, he is just drunk." "Be careful, Mr. Attorney." "You've been drinking!" Now, Sloane knew how some of his clients must have felt!

—

"Were we the de rippee or la ripper?" Larry's attempt at humor was well received by Thelma. For the first time since the robbery had occurred, Thelma felt nearly normal. "I'm not sure," she answered. "But one thing I do know." "What's that?" "Thank God, I married you!" "Why?" "I wouldn't have known what to do." Larry answered sincerely, "Well, if you weren't married to me, you might not have been there." "Oh, Larry!" "Do you think that the police will catch them?" "Hell no! By the time they are through typing up their reports and checking the lot, those clowns will be gone, long gone!"

—

Al Tedelset was not a known criminal. He was raised in Sumter, Pennsylvania by his grandparents. He was one of six children. In school, he had been reasonably studious, if not the brightest kid in the class. He left Sumter to find a different way of life in Atlanta. He stayed in Atlanta until one year ago when he journeyed south again, this time to Clearwater, Florida and then to his death. Al had one failing, envy. He resented his grandparents' constant refusal to become angry over alleged injustices. He began to hate those who achieved any modicum of success. Al Tedelset was deficient. He was awkward around women, tied by his early bonds to the church and his grandmother's admonitions. "What ever you do Al, keep your shirts clean." He scored his first piece of ass when he was fourteen. She was a maid. She literally took him. She could tell once they started his childlike foreplay, that he had never been there before. She was wise enough not to laugh at his rather fumbling efforts to achieve satisfaction. Al was in a strange euphoria. All that he had read and seen in spicy detectives and spicy adventures was now happening. The glow of animal warmth overwhelmed him. IT was over. She sighed and he wasn't sure. Suddenly his mind panicked. 10 days. 30 days. No period.

—

Vic Zabo left the lot. His thoughts of loyalty gone! He could easily be gone from Clearwater in an hour and gone from the specter of Al, Thelma and that feisty 45-year-old man to spoil the night! He saw a Waffle House. He slowed his walk. The purse! He would be a dead give away walking into the Waffle House with a ladies silver purse. Quickly he rifled the purse. A gas credit card, an American Express, a small rolled brush, three one dollar bills, 76 cents in change; the card, the brush and the money he pocketed. The wallet, the rings, he could look at in the Men's Room.

—

Larry Corvan was hungry. The excitement, the struggle, the strange sensual feeling, all combined to give him almost a spiritual appetite. "Honey, how about a sandwich?" Thelma, who opted for the kind of life she wanted, nodded in agreement. "What do you want; fried egg and bacon or bologna and cheese?" "Hell, I don't know. Maybe a bologna and cheese, it's easier." "How about some wine?" "Wine with bologna and cheese? Sure. Why not some St. Pierre?" Thelma laughed; she was now twice married, several times loved, and somehow felt at home with this person, who feared many and was feared by many. She set to her task, almost happily. The episode was not over, but it was, for the moment.

—

The D.C. 8 began a slow decent into Tampa International Airport. The stewardesses were busy collecting glasses, remnants of meals and advising those aboard to place their tray table in an upright position and return their seat back to the forward position. Samuel Tedelset looked weary as he sat pondering over his CC and water. Al—little Al. Whatever happened to him? Strange country, this Florida, many times he had wanted to come here but each time something interfered. Now he was here. For what … to bury his brother. Killed by some drunken attorney! Sam was an attorney.

(Flashback: The patrolman at the booking desk was making a phone call.)

Larry stopped midway in a bite as the phone rang again. "I hope it's not the kids." "Maybe it's the police?" she answered. The phone rang again, "Hello." "Mr. Corvan?" "Yes." "Sgt. Harrelson of the Clearwater PD." "Yes, Sgt.?" "We have an ID, I think, on the man you claim tried to hold you and your wife up this morning." "What do you mean tried to hold us up?" "Well sir, we don't know for sure that this is the man, but we think he may be." "What does he look like?" "Well sir that is hard to say," responded the Sgt., "he was run over by a car." "Where?" asked Larry. "In the Copper Koto parking lot." "What time?" "As near as we can tell 2:56 a.m." Sounding surprised, Larry said, "Really?" The officer gave an affirmative, "Yes."

—

Sloane registered a 0.11 on the Breathalyzer test. He was booked on DWI with a possible manslaughter charge. Pete Benson, assistant States Attorney, was called by the police department at 3:30 in the morning. He was not the most agreeable person in the world. When the phone rang, his wife Carolyn stirred and sat upright. Pete found the phone by Braille as she turned on the light. "Hello?" It was as much a question as a greeting. "Mr. Benson?" "Yes." "We may have a manslaughter case." "Well?" "Well sir, a Mr. Sloane." The officer was interrupted by Benson asking, "You mean Sloane, the attorney?" "Yes sir." Pete's head was beginning to clear. He and Carolyn had invited a few close friends over the night before for a small party. No hangovers, just a little hard to get started. "Have you booked him?" Benson asked. "Just on DWI." "Is he still there?" "Yes sir." "O.K., I'll be right down." Carolyn's face was concerned and quizzical. "Is Barry in trouble?" "It sure looks that way", answered her husband. "There is a possible manslaughter charge with DWI."

—

Pete Benson was young, 28 years old. He was average size, 5'10", and weighed about 178 pounds. Carolyn was waiting for more comments. Pete's mind was racing. Sloane was a member of a very powerful firm. He was very popular and somewhat powerful politically. He tried to kid himself that this would make no difference. It would.

—

Vic Zabo, hoping that his appearance did not belie the inner feeling, sat at the counter and ordered a waffle, one egg, a side of bacon, and coffee. He smiled at the waitress, a fifty-ish woman with streaks of gray in her head of hair, sitting on an overweight body with two gold teeth. She served the coffee. He took a quick sip, got off the stool and went to the men's room. Vic swung open the door of the john, closed and latched it. He pulled Corvan's wallet from his pocket. Okay, in cash, 50-60-100-200-300. Not bad. In fact, very good! In credit cards; Sunoco, Gulf, Fina, Triple A, and American Express. He turned it over, yep, there it was, Larry Corvan's signature. Perfect! Before American Express could catch up, he would be long gone and he had enough to get him home. He would look at the watch and rings later.

—

At 4:05 am, Pete Benson walked through the door of the police department. The Sgt. nodded and said, "Sloane is in that room on the left with his wife. We didn't lock him up." "Good," said Benson. No point in pushing, just yet. Benson pushed on the door, he wanted Sloane's story first. "Hey Barry, how are you feeling?" Sloane looking dazed replied, "Awful! A headache and a hangover." Benson proceeded to ask the necessary questions, "What happened?" Sloane looked Benson right in the eye and asked if the conversation was off the record. Benson stalled for an answer and finally agreed, yes it was off the record, he guessed. Disbelieving his answer, Sloane with pleading eyes said, "No, come on Pete! Either off the record or book me! You've already booked me for DWI. What I want to know is what about the manslaughter case? Off the record?" "Okay, okay, for the present." Pete's reply was a little irritated.

So Barry began his story. "Ok. We were leaving the club. We had a bet with Hugh and his wife that we could beat them home. You know Hugh … Hugh Swenson, the dermatologist. They live next door to us. The loser had to fix bacon and eggs. Well, I spotted this place between the parked cars that gave me a clear shot to the street, and being in a hurry I pulled through the space and felt the car run over something. I stopped, got out and there he was." "Who?" asked Benson. Sounding annoyed, Sloane said, "How the hell should I know! He was still under the car. My left wheel apparently went over his head and my right wheels went over his ankles. Most of him was under the car. I called for Hugh, but it was too late. He was gone. I had my wife call the police, while I checked to see if he was alive." "Was he?" "Hell, no! The weight of the Mark IV really squashed him. My God, Pete, I am not a killer!" For the first time, Benson felt real sympathy for a suspect. "Of course not, Barry, but it is a bad deal." Barry was beginning to crumble. As a lawyer, he was fighting himself as a citizen.

Meanwhile, Pete's mind was racing again. Well, he thought, what we have is a probable drunk, passed out, run over and killed by a person who has now been charged with DWI. There could and probably will be problems with family. Turning to Sloane, Benson said in his attorney voice, "Even if you beat any criminal charges, you may face some civil charges." Sobriety was more and more becoming to Barry. "All right, can my wife drive me home? I need to shower, change and get back down here after couple hours sleep. I mean, if I can?" Pete's answer to Barry was a serious, "No. Barry, from what you have told me, and if that information is correct, we need to do some serious talking." "Ah Pete, come on, I need some sleep. I need to try and get my head together and figure out what I'm into."

—

Sam Tengelstadt again eyed the stewardess with a certain amount of sexual interest. She was small, neatly packaged. She asked, "Another CC and water?" "Yes, please, and would you mind, with a small piece of lemon?" replied Sam. Sam, referred to by his colleagues as Uncle Sam, smiled and wished he was twenty-five again. His stewardess mentioned him to a co-worker, "He is a very nice man." That was Sam's curse.

—

Larry bit through the bologna and cheese while sipping his wine. Then he stopped abruptly, "Damn! Damn!" Thelma looked up from her book and asked, "What?" Larry said, "I forgot about the insurance. I should call them." Reminding her husband about the time, "You can't call them at 4:30 in the morning." Larry shook his head and agreed. The new day was only hours away. Thelma asked if he was going into work. "Yeah, I've got to be at the office by nine." "Well, finish your sandwich so you can get some sleep," remarked Thelma.

Vic Zabo was living high on the hog tonight. He found a lady for $50. Wow! He was really on. The broad was young, firm and bored. He was rich by his standards and she was satisfying by his standards. His life was the counter balance for twelve other human beings and no matter which way he moved, somebody had to lose.

Thelma scooped the coffee from the can and proceeded to partially fill the container at the top of the coffee maker. Larry was still asleep. This was a switch. Usually, Larry was up, retrieved the paper, skimmed the stories, made the coffee and was back in bed by six. She began her fantasy as she plugged in the coffee maker. *He was wordless, intense, and very determined. He had semi-raped her because she didn't want her purity impregnated.* No! She said to herself. Now is not the time or the place. Thoughts began to crisscross her mind. He is real (Larry). He is honest (not entirely). He is mine (true). She walked out to get the paper. Nothing in the paper. Of course not, she reasoned. The robbery was too late for the paper or T.V.

—

Barry Sloane retched, not food, flu, or booze. It was nerves! He had been warned about his entire lifestyle. His future was in real trouble. Okay, a DWI, which is not impossible. But manslaughter, that is something else. "Are you alright, Barry?" asked his wife. He said, "Sure, I always do this in the morning, talk out loud to myself." He was sarcastic but she missed it.

—

Vic Zabo had one thing on his mind … get out of town. Now Larry Corvan would help him. He smiled and said to the ticket lady, "One round trip ticket to Billings, please."

—

Sloane gargled, shaved and dressed for the day. No breakfast this morning. "Don't fix me anything", he called out to his wife. "You should have something," she voiced with concern. "No thanks." "How about some coffee?" "Not right now." He dressed methodically and went out to the kitchen. She was putting slices of bread into the toaster. Barry glanced at her and said, "I don't know what time I'll be back, but I'll call you as soon as I know something."

—

"Well, I can't tell anything much by the face but those appear to be the same clothes, he is about the same height. (There was a pause.) Yes, that's him." Larry Corvan was sure in his own mind that the crushed, lifeless form on the table in the pathology lab was the man who accosted him and his wife just ten hours earlier. "Are you absolutely sure?" asked Detective Lewis. "Yes, I'm as sure as I can be under these circumstances. I am sure that if he was alive and standing in a lineup, that I could identify him." "O.K.," replied Lewis. "Let's go back to the station and give your report." Back at the station Larry and Det. Lewis reviewed the report and made no changes. This report would be the focal point in Sloane's trial for manslaughter.

The final sensation; death, it did not miss. But he never really comprehended what was happening. His mouth already open and sucking air, filled with blood, broken teeth and tissue as the weight of the wheel crushed his skull. One eye left its socket. His tongue was ground in half. There was no further sensation. The brain, shocked from the massive weight, sent a final message … shock and death followed. There was no Presbyterian, pre-destination controlling this man. His fate had to be quick. The embalmer was going to have a hell of a job.

Larry Corvan arrived at his office a little flushed and excited over the past few hours. News of his physical prowess, not normally thought by most as his strong point, and the fact that the man was now dead, added a certain esteem and luster to Larry. He felt it. He also radiated it as a minor hero in a major way. His secretary looked unusually pert today. She was short, 5'1" small breasts, waist and hips, but nice. Someday, I'm going to have to check her out, thought Larry. Jackie, pert, pretty, and suddenly a little curious about her boss, followed him into his office. "Would you like a cup of coffee?" she asked. "Yeah, black," he answered. He smiled and she walked back to the outer office and prepared his coffee. She returned with the coffee and announced, "The afternoon meeting at 2 p.m. with the calendar people has been cancelled." "Damn," muttered Larry. He had that one figured to last the balance of the day. Well, there was plenty to do in the office. He looked up and smiled at his secretary. Damn, she was worth checking out.

CHAPTER NINE
Master of the Interview

From the Gordon Solie Collection

Gordon trying out his shoes in Frank Sinatra's footprints.

The Champion

He stands in the wings of the stage of life.

He is allied with time,

I hope he stands there as a friendly victor

For he will surely win

Don't anger him or your reward will be paid

Caress and accept his edict....

From the Gordon Solie Collection: photo by Jerry Prater

Two professional wrestling legends together: National Wrestling Alliance World Heavyweight Champion Lou Thesz (above left) and Gordon Solie (taking interview notes, above right). About three decades later, Gordon felt honored to be in the ring for Lou's Hall of Fame induction at WCW's Slamboree '93.

From the Gordon Solie Collection: photo by Gene Gordon © by Scooter Lesley

Jack Brisco (above right) won the NWA World Heavyweight Championship and later partnered with his brother Jerry to take the NWA World Tag Team Championship belts. Prior to his professional career, Jack won the 1965 NCAA national amateur wrestling championship, representing Oklahoma State University in the 191 poundage class. The studios lights were off (below) following three hours of production for the Saturday night *Georgia Championship Wrestling* show aired on WTBS. Jack watched intently as Gordon did the vocal cuts for the one hour show that appeared on Sunday.

From the Gordon Solie Collection: photo by Gene Gordon © by Scooter Lesley

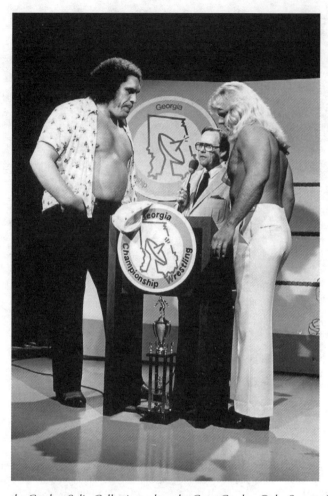

From the Gordon Solie Collection: photo by Gene Gordon © by Scooter Lesley

Andre the Giant (above left) won titles with the NWA, IWA and WWF on his way to becoming one of the most popular performers in the history of professional wrestling entertainment. Michael Hayes (above right) was a huge draw as one of the "Fabulous Freebirds."

Unequals

As human beings, we basically lack the intelligence to deal with affluence effectively. In our desire to make all men equal, we have lowered our over all productivity. We have become so involved in stating "I am as good as you" that we have forgotten that many are not.

From the Gordon Solie Collection: photo by Gene Gordon © by Scooter Lesley

In a 1989 Chicago match, Ricky "The Dragon" Steamboat (above left) took the NWA Heavyweight Championship.

From the Gordon Solie Collection: photo by Gene Gordon © by Scooter Lesley

Gordon held the microphone for Freddie Miller, who rushed onto the *Georgia Championship Wrestling* set to share his occasional "urgent message." Meanwhile, Mike Davis (above right) did his best to incite the studio audience.

From the Gordon Solie Collection: photo by Gene Gordon © by Scooter Lesley

Ted DiBiase (above right) spoke to Gordon while Jack Brisco looked on during a *Georgia Championship Wrestling* show. After winning titles in territories like Mid-South and the Central States, Ted went on to a successful career with the World Wrestling Federation.

In late 1959 and early 1960, "Iron" Mike DiBiase, Ted's father, had a good run as a "heel" in Tampa while feuding with Eddie Graham. Gordon covered the action with a microphone and also wrote about the "angles" in *Sports Shots with Solie*; "To call the television viewers 'free loadin' beer drinkers is hardly my way of expressing appreciation to the thousands of loyal wrestling fans that have been watching the matches each Saturday over WFLA-TV. 'Iron'

Mike, the present Southern Heavyweight Wrestling Champion, called the viewers just that on television last week. May I say this; we do not consider 'Iron' Mike or his opinion worth the powder to blow it you know where! He is a disgrace to the profession and should be barred. If you are wondering if I am bitter over the manhandling I received from him last week, you are exactly correct. I am mad, plenty mad, but I also realize that I am no match for a man as big as he is and a professional wrestler at that.

"I can only hope that one of the men who have challenged him will be able to beat him for the Southern Heavyweight Championship. I personally think the Red Raider was a better champion than this character from up north. He is certainly no credit to the profession or himself.

"His attitude toward the wrestling fan leaves much to be desired, and I for one, hope he loses his championship as quickly as possible. I have already filed a complaint to the Southern Wrestling Alliance, and I hope they will act on it in the near future.

"'Iron' Mike? Champion? Phooey! Promoter 'Cowboy' Luttrall and the entire staff of *The Sportscaster* want you to know that we appreciate your patronage, and we certainly do not agree or endorse the attitudes or actions of 'Iron' Mike."

Later, *The Sportscaster* featured "Iron" Mike a week after losing to Eddie Graham. Mike started screaming "foul," "conspiracy" and other accusations at Luttrall and the SWA. The satisfaction of beating "Iron" Mike was shadowed for Graham. Eddie Graham became more incensed by the insults, and the behavior of "Iron" Mike. "He is a big blabber mouth with a sadistic streak where his brain should be," said Graham in an interview. Graham continued, "He is a discredit to the profession and certainly an outlaw in society."

Gordon added his two cents worth in his column, "I certainly wish now that Eddie and Mike would shake hands and end this ever deepening and dangerous feud. It has become a situation here in Tampa that borders on mayhem of the worst sort. I sure hope that Eddie takes the title tonight, and that then we have possibly seen the last of 'Iron' Mike. Men of his ilk are not needed in the wrestling profession or in any other profession far as that goes. His kind is savage and only understands one thing … VIOLENCE. One thing for sure, win, lose, or draw, 'Iron' Mike will get all the violence he could ever ask for tonight against Eddie Graham. Don Curtis is still one of the finest wrestlers I have ever seen. It is too bad that he was unable to cop the title last week from Killer Kowalski."

Curtis got the shot at the World Champion, Kowalski, after he took the Southern Heavyweight title from DiBiase. Mike DiBiase thought he was going to wrestle Graham, and then Curtis showed up in the ring instead. Afterwards, a furious DiBiase was heard to say, "This is the greatest robbery since Jesse James was robbing trains. That peroxided bandit who calls himself a wrestler is too chicken to meet me in the ring, and has to call on that skeleton, Don Curtis, to substitute for him. I don't think Graham was hurt at all. I think he was too yellow to meet me in the ring, and I know he and Curtis and that so called Promoter Luttrall set me up for a patsy."

"Iron" Mike also had a definite opinion about his next main event opponent, Don Eagle. "I'll run this redskin back to his reservation in Canada, and when I do, I am going to force Luttrall to give me a shot at that yellow belly Eddie Graham," explained Mike.

(Note) To some readers it might appear that Gordon didn't care for "Iron" Mike DiBiase. Other readers might perceive that Gordon was simply promoting professional wrestling by "putting over" the "heel".

From the Gordon Solie Collection: Photo by Gene Gordon © by Scooter Lesley

The Funk brothers, Terry (above left) and Dory, Jr. (above right), both won the National Wrestling Alliance World Heavyweight Championship during their illustrious careers. Tommy Rich (below right) was recognized as the NWA World Heavyweight Champion in 1981.

From the Gordon Solie Collection: Photo by Gene Gordon © by Scooter Lesley

Something Left Behind

From the Gordon Solie Collection: photo by Gene Gordon © by Scooter Lesley

Leroy Brown (above left) spoke while Gordon and "Big Red" Reece looked on. One day when Gordon mentioned the cold weather, Reece responded by taking off his own coat and putting it on Gordon. "There Mr. Solie," said Reece, "now you're not cold anymore." Gordon answered with something like, "This is not a coat. It's a tent!"

From the Gordon Solie Collection: photo by the Gene Gordon © by Scooter Lesley

From left to right above: Ole Anderson, Gordon, "Mr. Wrestling II" (Johnny Walker), and Steve Travis. Ole and "Mr. Wrestling II" were two of the biggest stars during Gordon's career with *GCW*. Travis was crowned as the Georgia Television Champion in 1980.

Prime Gone

The age of fifty does many things.
It makes a fool of most men.
It wets their desire and stifles their ability.
It succors their ego and deflates their masculinity.
How many extra cups of coffee or drinks of brandy
To win the favor of a pat on the cheek?

This point in time … is gone.

From the Gordon Solie Collection: photo by Gene Gordon © by Scooter Lesley

Gordon admired the "charisma" of Dusty Rhodes (above right). Dusty showed his National Wrestling Alliance Heavyweight Championship belt won from Harley Race on August 21, 1979, in Tampa, Fla.

From the Gordon Solie Collection: photo by Gene Gordon © by Scooter Lesley

Dick Slater looked like he was ready to explode as he talked about the Georgia Heavyweight Championship belt. It was a hotly contested belt as Dick gained title victories over the "Spoiler," "Mr. Wrestling II," and Paul Jones in the mid-'70s.

From the Gordon Solie Collection: photo by Gene Gordon © by Scooter Lesley

Harley Race (above left) discussed one of his many NWA title belts with Gordon on *GCW*. The two men worked together until Gordon's final years, including some shows for Karl Lauer's *World Legion Wrestling* in the late 1990s.

From the Gordon Solie Collection: photo by Gene Gordon © by Scooter Lesley

During 1982, the "Masked Superstar" (Bill Eadie, above left) and "Super D" (Scott Irwin, above right) took custody of the NWA National Tag Team Championship belts in Columbus, Ga.

From the Gordon Solie Collection: photo by Gene Gordon © by Scooter Lesley

When *Championship Wrestling from Georgia* promoted live shows outside the state, a need arose for different titles. It didn't make sense to have a Georgia heavyweight belt, for example, defended at a show in the Ohio Center in Columbus, Ohio. A decision was made to unify the Georgia title with the existing National title. The NWA National Heavyweight title belt was displayed, above right, by the "Masked Superstar" (Bill Eadie).

From the Gordon Solie Collection: photo by Gene Gordon © by Scooter Lesley

Don Jardine (above left) wrestled as "The Spoiler" when he competed except in the Mid-Atlantic where he was known as "Super Destroyer." "The Spoiler" won the NWA National Heavyweight title in Wheeling, W. Va., and again in Atlanta, Ga.

From the Gordon Solie Collection: photo by Gene Gordon © by Scooter Lesley

Buddy Colt (above left) won belts in the Central States and tore a path of title victories through the Southeastern United States. Roger Kirby (above right) helped Buddy defeat Ole and Gene Anderson in November of 1974 for the Georgia Tag Team title.

Something Left Behind

From the Gordon Solie Collection: photo by Gene Gordon © by Scooter Lesley

From left to right above: Manager Rock Hunter, Pak Song, Gordon and Abdullah the Butcher. While Rock made claims about what his tag team was going to do, Abdullah repeatedly hit himself in the head with a shovel. After putting down the shovel, Abdullah turned and slowly poured out Gordon's coffee. Then he ate Gordon's coffee cup! With regard to Rock's comments and his cup, Gordon went to a break with something like, "And that remains to be seen. I'm going to go get a little coffee. We'll be right back." No matter what happened on the set, Gordon never seemed to get rattled. That may be why Houston wrestling promoter, Paul Boesch, referred to Gordon as "the calm amidst the storm."

The 275-pound Korean, Pak Song, was on hand when "Miss Lillian" Carter, mother of former President Jimmy Carter, visited Columbus, Ga., to watch the wrestlers in action. Song was pictured in the *Decatur Daily* along with "Miss Lillian," Tommy Rich, Bob Armstrong, Tony Atlas, Charlie Cook, "Mr. Wrestling II" and Dick Slater on January 20, 1978.

From the Gordon Solie Collection: photo by Gene Gordon © by Scooter Lesley

Former National Football League player, Ernie Ladd (above left) used to bust Gordon's chops when he came on the set of *GCW* with words like, "Shut up, Mr. Solie! You're just a television announcer talking out of the side of your neck … yick, yick, yick … yonk, yonk, yonk! Nobody wants to hear what you have to say! They want to hear the king, and *I'm* the king! Not like that criminal, 'Mr. Wrestling II,' who hides behind a mask!"

Stirring things up wasn't exactly new for Ernie. In October of 1971, *The Rassler* reported that Ladd was in a feud with Johnny Valentine and refused a $1000 check from Buddy Wolfe to opt out of the match. Ernie and Johnny were suddenly the main event in front of wrestling fans at the North Side Coliseum in Fort Worth, Texas.

From the Gordon Solie Collection: photo by Gene Gordon © by Scooter Lesley

A large man at 6'2" tall and around 320 pounds packed on his frame, Stan Hansen was popular with the *Georgia Championship Wrestling* fans. In addition to Georgia titles, Stan won titles in the Pacific Wrestling Federation and the AWA (American Wrestling Association). He also had the most significant victories for a "gaijin" or a foreigner as referred to by the Japanese, when he became the first such man to defeat the Asian great, Antonio Inoki, and also the "Giant" Baba.

From the Gordon Solie Collection: photo by Gene Gordon © by Scooter Lesley

"Mr. Wrestling" (above left) in his white ring jacket with "Mr. Wrestling II" (above center). Tim Woods, aka "Mr. Wrestling," started winning titles as an amateur with Big Ten Championships representing Michigan State University in 1958 and 1959. In addition to winning tag team titles with "Mr. Wrestling," Johnny Walker ("Mr. Wrestling II") won the Georgia Heavyweight belt on ten different occasions.

From the Gordon Solie Collection: photo by Gene Gordon © by Scooter Lesley

Terry Gordy (above left), Michael Hayes (above center) and Buddy Robert (above right) won Georgia Tag Team titles and NWA National Tag Team championships as the "Fabulous Freebirds." Buddy also teamed with Jerry Brown to form the "Hollywood Blonds" under the management of "Sir Oliver Humperdink."

From the Gordon Solie Collection: photo by Gene Gordon © by Scooter Lesley

"Sterling Golden" (above right) went on to break attendance records and become the biggest name in professional wrestling entertainment as "Hulk Hogan."

John Thomas

John Thomas, John Thomas
Stood alone, proud and strong
John Thomas, John Thomas
God for a moment
John Thomas, John Thomas
King for the hour
John Thomas, John Thomas
Enters the heavenly bower
John Thomas, John Thomas
Not defeated but spent
John Thomas, John Thomas
From heaven has went
John Thomas, John Thomas
Can return again
The beginning and end

From the Gordon Solie Collection: photo by Gene Gordon © by Scooter Lesley

Gordon held the microphone while Ric Flair shared some thoughts with the studio audience and the television viewers for a *Georgia Championship Wrestling* show. In addition to countless TV appearances together, Gordon and Ric worked together at live events including "Lords of the Ring" at the Orange Bowl in Miami, Fla., and "Night of Champions at the Meadowlands" at the Brendan Byrne Arena in East Rutherford, N.J.

From the Gordon Solie Collection: photo by Gene Gordon © by Scooter Lesley

Sixteen-time world champion, "Nature Boy" Ric Flair (above left), held his National Wrestling Alliance World Heavyweight Championship belt during an interview with Gordon.

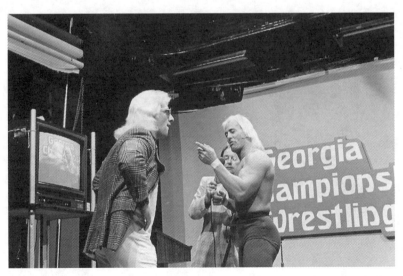

From the Gordon Solie Collection: photo by Gene Gordon © by Scooter Lesley

Ric Flair (above left) seemed to take exception to some strong words from Austin Idol (above right).

Something Left Behind

From the Gordon Solie Collection: photo by Gene Gordon © by Scooter Lesley

From left to right above: Ivan Koloff, Ole Anderson, Gordon, Tommy Rich and Wahoo McDaniel. The four grapplers were in a heated discussion about the Georgia Tag Team Championship.

From the Gordon Solie Collection: photo by Gene Gordon © by Scooter Lesley

Bob Armstrong (above center) spoke with Gordon about the NWA National Tag Title that he and his son Brad (above right) won in Atlanta on November 25, 1981.

From the Gordon Solie Collection: photo by Gene Gordon © by Scooter Lesley

When a studio match ended prematurely and the program needed to fill a few minutes, it was time to bring out the "stretcher," Terry Funk (above right). Terry not only filled the available air time, he could heat up the place in a hurry with a slow ranting like: "I'm tired and I've got a headache … I was just told my plane is delayed … and I have to spend three more hours in this stinky, nasty, rotten, peach-tree smelling town … I should be at home in my beautiful state of Texas." Of course, the Georgia folks didn't take kindly to his words and reacted with some sentiments of their own.

From the Gordon Solie Collection: photo by Gene Gordon © by Scooter Lesley

"Bruiser" Brody fired up fans as a big time "heel" in route to twice carrying the NWA American Heavyweight title.

From the Gordon Solie Collection: photo by Gene Gordon © by Scooter Lesley

Terry Taylor (above left), Steve "O" (second from right), and Les Thornton (far right) were on hand as Gordon closed the show with his familiar, "This is Gordon Solie saying so long … from the Peachtree State of Georgia."

From the Gordon Solie Collection: photo to Gordon from Carol Hasson

Jimmy Golden (above right) was in Gordon's face trying to make a point. Along with his cousin, Robert Fuller (above left), Jimmy won tag team titles under *Southeastern Championship Wrestling* and *Continental Championship Wrestling*. Both men were raised around the wrestling industry. Robert's father, Buddy Fuller, was from the Welch family and promoted *Gulf Coast Championship Wrestling* with another relative, Lee Fields. Later in his career, Robert entertained fans as "Colonel Parker." Jimmy Golden's father, Billy Golden, promoted wrestling in central Alabama based out of Montgomery.

As for Gordon, in a television broadcasting career spanning 36 years, he called more than 15,000 professional wrestling matches averaging out to 416 matches per year. Equally as impressive was his mastery of the interview.

From the Gordon Solie Collection

Gordon looked fearful as "Sir Oliver Humperdink" tried to get in the middle and calm down an irate Terry Funk on the set of *FCW (Florida Championship Wrestling)*.

CHAPTER TEN
Another Road to Rome

One Week from Rome

Since the beginning, man has always striven for Utopia. Each time he reaches out to grasp it in his own limited thinking, it is torn from his grasp by the less-civilized savage. Note I say less civilized, for certainly man in any form is still savage. Yet each time man has Utopia ripped from his bosom, the next generation has a little less traveling to do to make his bid for the end of perfection.

The great days of Athens … the smoldering era of Pompeii … the rise and fall of the Roman Empire … Portugal and her empires … France and her folly… England … where the sun never sets … all measures of Utopia. But for how long … Hitler and his Nietzschean theory of Superman; where do stand they now?

History tells us in cold black print and time tells us in rolling cemetery hills. Where stand us … America? How do we compare with the greatness and stature of the Roman era … of England … of France … of Germany? Reflect with me for a moment some comparisons that necessarily rule my thinking.

Our laws, basically Roman … our architectures … many examples of Romanism. Our religion … most certainly latter-day Roman. The seat of the original church is still in Rome. Ah! You say, there is all the further you can pursue this thought. Certainly we do not have the Roman taste for blood … the days of the great gladiators … the Amphitheaters … no, not on the same level. No, we are not as honest about our bloodletting now as the Romans were. Now we allow mass slaughter on the highways … we now call them accidents. Unavoidable, I believe is the phrase.

Occasionally, our hypocritical sense of moral values allows us to outwardly punish some survivors of a battle of the steel coffins. Mostly, however, we are inclined to be lenient in the final analysis because we know deep-down inside we, too, may join the ranks this minute.

But what about our scientific advances? Certainly no one can dispute that we are the greatest country in the world. Russia took exception and then proved the exception. We are the largest Christian country in the world. There is no dispute there, now is there? Of course not! But how many real "honest" to "God" Christians do you know? What about yourself? Are you a Christian? Why? Why not? Kindly liken our present day U.S.A. with the grandeur of Rome. Like the sign of the bear to Attila the Hun. Do you see by any stretch of the imagination a parallel? Can you see a possibility, however remote, that we too with all our mass production, our scientific "know how," our great Christian brotherhood, could fall. Of course not! That happens to the other fellow, not us, like cancer, auto accidents, heart attacks and the other catastrophes that eventually take us all. Then why not our country, too!

Is it true….could we be ONE WEEK FROM ROME?

A Fairy Tale

Once upon a time there were two great and honorable kings. Each king was known for his goodness and wisdom in the manner in which he treated his subjects. These two kings were also thought of highly by all the smaller neighboring kingdoms. These smaller kingdoms were often helped by the larger domains with grants, etc.

Now, although these two kings were very wise, they let some evil men into positions of high honor in their respective kingdoms. These evil men immediately began to plot against all the other kingdoms, and tried to convince the smaller domains that the larger kingdoms were trying to hurt them. Pretty soon the smaller kingdoms began to fight amongst themselves, and the larger kingdoms in order to protect them brought them into protective custody. Before long the two large kingdoms had surrounded themselves with little satellite kingdoms, and it looked as though they were finally going to have to fight each other.

One day a fairy godfather appeared on the scene and granted each king two wishes. Upon the advice of the two evil men in each kingdom, the kings wished the other dead, and that they would rule the other kingdom. The fairy godfather granted their wishes, and the two kings died, and the evil men took over the kingdoms.

Because these men were evil, they immediately went to war against each other, and soon all the people in the two kingdoms were dead except the two evil men. They in turn killed each other, and then nobody was left.

IT IS BETTER TO RULE IN HARMONY THAN TO DIE IN DISCORD.

From the Gordon Solie Collection: photo from "The Grapevine" © by Jerry Prater/Grapevine Publishing

Gordon and Eddie Graham (above right) on the set of *CWF*

From the Gordon Solie Collection

Les Thatcher (above left), Bobby Shane (above center), and Gordon were entertaining the television viewers during the Atlanta promotional wars. Gordon continued at the microphone with *Georgia Championship Wrestling* for 12 years.

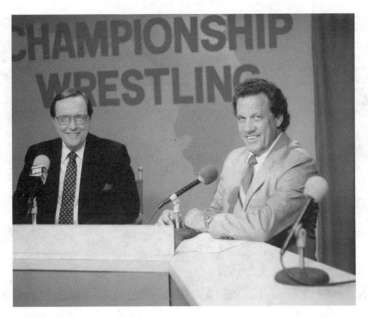

From the Gordon Solie Collection: photo from "The Grapevine" © by Jerry Prater/Grapevine Publishing

Gordon and co-host Buddy Colt, above right, on *CWF* in the 1980s

From the Gordon Solie Collection: photo by Gene Gordon © by Scooter Isley

"Rowdy" Roddy Piper, above right, co-hosted with Gordon on *Georgia Championship Wrestling* in the early 1980s.

From the Gordon Solie Collection: photo to Gordon from Carol Hasson

Gordon did a limited number of televised shows in Dothan, Ala., and Knoxville, Tenn., for *Southeastern Championship Wrestling* in the 1970s, but became a regular on *Continental Championship Wrestling* in 1985. In the picture below, Gordon received a smooch while "Diamond" Dallas Page and "Sir Oliver Humperdink" watched with interest on the set of *Florida Championship Wrestling*.

From the Gordon Solie Collection

To Henry's Pond

In success there is deep mockery
The frustration of too much….
The still specter of failure….
The incomprehensible design of disaster….
Is there a measure?
To be sure….
Walden's Pond!

The Game

To cope with total egomania….
Coupled with complete ruthlessness
Becomes … myopic in one's approach to the day by day of business acumen
One slowly … but so slowly realizes … chess is played at all levels.
Death is the only victor.

CHAPTER ELEVEN
Starting Anew

Too Much

Too much hypocrisy

Too much government

Too much ill health

Too many lonely people

Too many overpaid under achievers who only know

Corporate politics.

Too many cracks in societal platforms for people to slip

Through and get lost in too many stupid bureaucratic files.

Too many who consider loyalty a weakness and not a strength.

Too many who consider the lie superior to the truth!

From the Gordon Solie Collection: photo by Ronald C. Thomas, Jr.

Tracy Smothers, one of "The Southern Boys," fired up the fans before a match in Panama City, Fla.

From the Gordon Solie Collection: photo by Ronald C. Thomas, Jr.

The "Tonga Kid" looked determined to keep his opponent down.

From the Gordon Solie Collection: photo by Ronald C. Thomas, Jr.

The "Iron Sheik" signaled to the crowd that he was No. 1 at a 1990 NWA show in Panama City, Fla.

From the Gordon Solie Collection

In 1995, Gordon became the first non-wrestler inducted into the WCW Hall of Fame. Even in retirement, however, Gordon stayed involved in wrestling as an officer for the Florida NWA, an announcer for Ring Warriors (Eurosport internet wrestling program translated into six languages), a board member for Cauliflower Alley Club(CAC), and hosted some shows for Karl Lauer's *World Legion Wrestling.* Karl was Chairman, Vice President of CAC when Gordon set another first for a pro wrestling announcer; Gordon was inducted into the Cauliflower Alley Club Hall of Fame.

Gordon's contributions that began with radio interviews of professional wrestlers in 1950, ended in the spring of 2000 when he resigned from his last board position … 50 years promoting the squared circle.

Post Wrestling Depression
December 1995

It has now been over six months since I have absented myself from the pro wrestling arena, and I am beginning to understand the meaning of post wrestling depression. I thought I could handle the freedom of not having to meet a deadline, and the joy of waking on the morrow without the specter of having to travel to Atlanta to do a job I could no longer justify. WRONG-OH, boy was I wrong!!!! I am not the almighty watchdog of this bit of show business humanity, but I must admit I still hold a great deal of pride regarding my participation in the sport. It is now common knowledge that promoters of today select a definite role for a wrestler to portray in their new organization, but they also pick out a character identifying name for him to alert the public that Sam Jones is about to take on a fictional character and Jim Smith....

Fictitious names and the like are o.k. if you are a movie star and you are playing a role ... but as an alleged athlete ... I think not!! Ah, hah, you say ... that's what we always believed anyway ... so be it ... but that does not take away their athletic prowess ... it merely verifies to all of us that anyone can take on another persona.

The original prelude written by Gordon for a wrestling book is shown below.

Prelude

My life has been a series of fragmentations ... from birth till now ... I have fragmented my relationships with everyone that I have known ... I suppose it really began when I was born, but I don't want to belabor the popular theory of "well it was my parents fault"... hell ... they were having a tough enough time trying to get along without the burden of some little bundle of joy ... I was born the year the Stock Market crashed ... I didn't know about it for years ... and certainly didn't understand it for decades ... I will attempt in the next few hundred pages to "defrag" my natural computer to try to give you an insight into the most intriguing sport this world has ever seen ... the world of professional wrestling ... THE FAKE ... THE FRAUD ... THE MOST UNFORGIVING SPORT IN THE WORLD ... and I might add to all of you ... the most suspect sport ... short of course of the Black Sox scandal ... the collegiate basketball points shaving reports ... the NFL fixing ... the fixing of horse racing ... dog racing ... boxing matches, you name it ... should we talk about politics? Or should we talk about religion? You name it ... it can be fragmented. I will not take on that task in this missile. I will merely try to defrag my life and maybe be able to give you a cleaner and more precise view of the sport that has been my joy, my child, my heartache, my adult life, my income and my judgment of an honest hypocrisy ... one, that after you finish ... you might realize ... we are all hypocrites in one form or another ... enough of that for the moment ... let me get back to the point ... fragmentation ... my life began fragmented ... my mother and my father were divorced before I was two years old..."as far as I know," and I was adopted when I was about nine years old. As long as I can remember ... I was taught to dislike my biological father ... what a mistake for anyone to do to their child; it too would come back to haunt me later in life ... Enough for now....

I remain,

Gordon Solie

Full Circle

The cycle is almost complete

We have progressed to the point of oblivion

We no longer hear the songs of nature portrayed by the birds

Nor do we see the spreading wings of the love making blue jays

To live we must return to the earth and sea

Let us welcome oblivion and start anew

The Awares

Why do we cling so tenaciously to life?

Because it is the only thing we know?

If this be the answer then explain life

There are but three classes of people

Those who are not aware

Those who wish to be aware

And those who are aware

Only the latter lives

And he lives only by dying

Hope

If I have somehow expressed….

A fear, a philosophy or a frustration or acceptance

That you have known or understand

Then I am not alone.

From the Gordon Solie Collection

In 1986, Joe Pedicino began as executive producer for an innovative and popular professional wrestling news program aired on WATL-TV in Atlanta, Ga. The new show, *Pro Wrestling This Week* featured two hosts; Joe Pedicino and Gordon Solie.

Lord of the Microphone (excerpt)
By Bill Apter

"When the world lost Gordon Solie on July 29, 2000, a huge piece of pro wrestling was taken to the grave with him and that piece is called 'credibility.' Gordon Solie was the master when it came to bringing that same credibility to all of us whom had their pro wrestling experiences shaped by his marvelous broadcasting during our lifetimes."

TO MY GRANDFATHER AND FRIEND
Something Left Behind

Wandering through a dessert,
Once full of life,
I stop to look,
At flowering plants,
Plants like children,
Rushing up and into the world.
Now I understand,
What my grandfather saw …
When he looked at me
With that all-knowing smirk.
He saw the world,
Not for the cruelness outside,
But for the never-ending life.
The desert is a desert,
Only to the untrained eye.
Underneath is a fountain of life,
Springing up unchallenged.
When I quicken my pace,
I see my true inheritance
As that smirk takes form once more …
On my own wandering face.

By Jameson Parker Allyn

So for now, as he would say;
"This is Gordon Solie saying; so long from the Sunshine State."

Biography (Credentials)

Relevant experience: Gordon Solie

Radio:
- WEBK Radio; rhythm and blues show, sports show interviewing professional athletes
- WFLA Radio; co-host of sports show with Milt Spencer
- WPLA Radio; sports announcer
- University of Tampa; station manager and DJ
- WTSP Radio; host of the hit show, *A Salute to Havana*
- WYOU Radio; sports director

Stock car racing:
- Speedway Park; announcer, amateur race driver
- Florida State Fairgrounds; announcer for the annual IMCA races
- McDill Air Force Base; announcer for stock car races
- Dery Sports Promotions; racing announcer and PR man for Phillips Field and Plant Field
- Golden Gate Speedway; part owner, announcer, general manager
- Automobile Racing Commissioner of Ybor City
- Supreme Secretary General of Sports Announcers of Ybor City
- Sunshine Speedway; president
- Suncoast Speedways, Inc; president and PR man for three race tracks

Movies:
- Technical director for two feature-length racing films

Thrill shows:
- Three years as announcer for the Thrillcade throughout the USA and Canada

Professional Wrestling:
- Deep South Sports; Ring announcer and P/R man
- Championship Wrestling from Florida; TV host
- Georgia Championship Wrestling (TBS); TV host
- Global Wrestling; TV host
- Southeastern Championship Wrestling; TV host
- Continental Championship Wrestling; TV host
- Pro Wrestling This Week; TV host
- World Pro Wrestling from Japan; host for two part series.
- Global Wrestling Alliance; TV host
- Florida Championship Wrestling; TV host
- Wrestling News Network; news segment host on NWA Power Hour
- NWA Pay Per Views; interviews
- Clash of the Champions; interviews
- World Wide Wrestling; TV host
- WCW Pro Wrestling; TV host
- Sports Radio Network; news segment host
- Ring Warriors; Eurosport internet wrestling show host; translated into six different languages
- World Legion Wrestling; TV host

Charities:
- Police Athletic League; publicity
- Florida Sheriff's Association; honorary lifetime member (Sheriff's Boys Ranch)
- Babe Zaharias Sports Week; chairman
- American Cancer Society, Hillsborough County; board member
- Muscular Dystrophy; emcee for telethon
- Division of Youth Services
- MISD (Muscular Injuries and Skeletal Disease); board member
- Tampa Bay Buccaneers and Pro Wrestlers charity softball; voice of the wrestlers
- Leukemia Society of America, Suncoast Chapter; board member

- NCAA Soccer National Championship
- United Cerebral Palsy
- Big Brothers/Big Sisters of Tampa Bay
- SERVE (School Enrichment Resource Volunteers in Education Honors)
- Florida Child's Wish Come True, Inc; board member
- Cauliflower Alley Club; board member and emcee

Writing Experience:
- Newspapers:

  Stringer for *The Ledger, The Tampa Times, The Tampa Tribune, La Gaceta,* and *The Temple Terrace Times*
- Racing:

  Wrote the promotional pieces and press releases for race tracks for 12 years
- Professional Wrestling:

  Wrote promotional pieces for 20 years; wrote a column for *The Sportscaster,* wrote a column for *The Ringsider,* wrote athlete bios for televised events; wrote and produced his own wrestling annual
- Radio:

  Wrote and produced his own radio shows, wrote award-winning radio editorials

Other:
- *Tampa Bay Sports*; wrote column entitled *Sports Slants by Solie*
- *Checkered Flag*; Gordon wrote this column under the pen name, Axel Geare
- *Inside the Squared Circle*; Gordon and Douglas Daudt wrote a two-hour documentary for a network broadcast
- Gordon was a producer for stadium-size wrestling events. One example was *Superbrawl* for WCW and Turner Broadcasting Systems, Inc. in 1991.